Vedic Concept of Biosphere

(The Secret of Creation)

Dr. C. P. Trivedi

Originals
(an imprint of Low Price Publications)
Delhi-110052

Distributed by
D.K. Publishers Distributors (P) Ltd.
4834/24, Ansari Road, Darya Ganj,
New Delhi-110002
Phones: 51562573, 51562575, 51562578
e-mail: dkpd@del3.vsnl.net.in
visit us at: www.dkpd.com

First Published 2006

ISBN 81-88629-46-4

Published by
Originals
(an imprint of Low Price Publications)
A-6, Nimri Commercial Centre,
Near Ashok Vihar Phase-IV, Delhi-110052
Phones: 27302453
e-mail: lpp@nde.vsnl.net.in
visit us at: www.lppindia.com

Printed at
D K Fine Art Press P Ltd.
Delhi-110052

PRINTED IN INDIA

Dr. Bal Ram Jakhar

GOVERNOR MADHYA PRADESH

RAJ BHAVAN
BHOPAL-462 003

Foreword

Dr. C.P. Trivedi's Book on Vedic Concept of Biosphere (The Secret of creation) is a monumental work on Veda, which has the potentiality to give new dimension to the Indian culture. To interpret the Vedic hymns has been a great puzzle for the scholars. Authored with deep inquest and intellect, the book is a rich addition to the available Vedic literature. It gives a scientific interpretation of Vedas, revealing the fact that Vedic culture was much more advanced than our present day civilization The testimony of the same can be traced in the origin of life and the theory of Karmik rebirth about which the modern scientists are still in dark. Dr. Trivedi has discussed the Vedic principles pertaining to ecological principles, Laws of Thermodynamics Genetics and photosynthesis in Vedic hymns, which shows that we can extract much more from the Vedic hymns for the global cooperation and world peace as indicated in the Vedic concept **Vasudhaiv Kutumbakam**, the whole world is our family. I congratulate Dr. C.P. Trivedi for his outstanding contribution on Veda as a professor and a scientist. I hope The book will be widely popular.

(Bal Ram Jakhar)

Contents

Preface

It is a fact that after the independence Indian youth and people with education are feeling a gap between the old culture and the modern thoughts. A Nation should have a proud of his own Culture, accordingly the National feeling is the back bone of a Nation. But in India after independene we have considered the culture as a religion, although the India has a great tradition and the cultural heritage unparallel in the world. Which has the capacity to lead and give new light to the world. On the contrary the intellectuals and the scientists sometimes feel guilty cauntious about the superstitious culture to which they belongs, accordinglly the brain drain is there from India.

It is only during my Ph.D. on Environmental pollution, which was a burning problem at that time and was able to give me an intellectual push being a pioneer worker in the field. But my desire to do something new, I have asked to my respected Dr. S.S. Nigam to give some stanza from the Vedic literature about the pollution, he has given me few stanza, which I have used in my thesis, it has given me a new direction for thinking on the Veda and I have started working on the Environmental problems and Indian culture with an aim to find the scientific facts. My traditional knowledge of the Vedic culture, Astrology and the knowledge of modern ecology have given me the guidelines for the interpretation of the Vedic hymns, my respected prof. L.P. Mall has encouraged me. The subject which I was teaching to the post graduate classes has given me a deep insight into the Vedic hymns.The Vedic knowledge is in the form of metaphors and the riddles, along with this the seers have raised the questions and have given the answers in the form of questions, which is known as *Brahmodya charchā* or intellectual discussion.

"Vedas are symbol of India and Indian culture, the position, which India have in the world is due to its glorious past and in turn world expect that India may take lead with its glorious cultural heritage." These are the views of a German Journalist, who was commenting on India's development in the field of science and technology. These words have given a push and I have started a mission to trace the key for interpretation of theVedic hymns. I was surprise to see that the western scholars have done a lot of work for Indian culture, through different commentaries on the Veda and other Religious scriptures but with their own limitations. The same has given me a new insight in to the Vedic hymns, ultimately after a long journey of twenty five years in the field. I have been able to trace the key of Vedic hymns and reached to the conclusion that the Vedic literature is a example of cryptographic art and skill. Where the words and verses are cryptic having a vast ocean of knowledge behind it, which can be only expressed after reaching at the climax of the development. The basic theme behind it is the human psychology that the human beings understand the language of human beings. As such the Vedic seers have used the imaginary man in a anthropomorphic manner to reveal the truth through it. Where words or names of the deities indicates towards a phenomena of nature.

The knowledge of the Vedic hymns move around the basic principles of the creation.

It seems that the fundamental energy is the original source of the creation, from where the different components of the nature have been synthesized, through energy transformation under temperature pressure gradient. The first cell is get synthesized in the water at its own under natural conditions. With energy transformation in side a closed system it has acquired a life energy, this energy can be generated due to the streaming of the protoplasm and the movements of the charged particles in side a closed system. This energy, which is being generated due to the movements of the charged particles, it is the first symbol of life. With the evolution of living beings in the nature, the life energy is also having its evolution, which gradually attains stability in the young cells with metabolic reactions, it under go gradually towards its end, through aging of the cells.

With the evolution of multi cellular organisms, the life energy is having a common appearance. The evolution of the living beings and their various forms are due to the evolution of the DNA base sequence with complexity of genetic code. It means for the whole external evolution of the living beings. The DNA is the main genetic material, which maintains its continuity in the living beings and carries the hereditary characters from one generation to the another generation. In this way the DNA regulates the course of life through the hereditary characters in the living beings. The streaming of the protoplasm in the living cells is the source of life energy, which gets further strength through movement of the sap in plants and circulation of blood in the animals. In human beings and the higher animals it gets further strength with evolution through the development of nervous system. Their movements and metabolic functions in the body enhance the production of life driving energy, which acts as its food. Which undergo deterioration with aging and ultimately get seized with inactivity of the concern organs. In this way there are two centers in the body one is DNA and other is life energy, both are important for life and independent for their function. The same has been indicated in *the Ṛgveda* and *Upanishads.*

Two birds with fair wings, knit with bonds of friendship, in the same sheltering tree have found refuge, one of the twin eats the sweet Fig-tree's fruitage; the other eating not regardeth only.

It indicates that the life energy is a spectator and the DNA is a biosoul, who enjoy the fruit of life.

After tracing all the above facts and their role in the creation, the Vedic seers have formulated their knowledge in the form of metaphors and riddles in the Vedic hymns.

The other important facts about the creation have been incorporated in the ritualistic cults of sacrifice, where the process, through which creation came in to existence has been preserved symbolically through the preparation of the sacrificial altar - *Yagnyavedi*. The facts about the **'Origin of life'** have been incorporated in the hymns related with *Rbhu* (cell) as a celestial race, The life on the earth is due to the presence of ozone layer in the atmosphere, which absorbs toxic Ultraviolet rays, it has been expressed in the creation hymns as a protector. The most important event in the history of life on the earth is the conversion of light energy in to the chemical energy **(Photosynthesis)**, the same has been incorporated in the wedding hymns with a symbolic expression through the ritualistic cults during the marriage. The other most important event in the life is death on the earth's surface, the same has been incorporated in the funeral hymns. Where it has been indicated that life and death on the earth's surface are under a cyclic phenomena, during which, human beings prepares them selves for the next journey with mental evolution. For which DNA is the main factor, who carries the information from one generation to another generation. Who keeps the record of one's own deeds in its genetic code language. The code is univeral, the same has been indicated through *Yama* **(Chromosomes,** which have the information about the life and death in its **DNA-(Deoxy Ribose Nucleic Acid)**. Yama has been termed as God of death. His messengers are the two dogs, the sons of *Saramā*, four eyed and brindled. The two dogs represents two strips of the DNA double helix and the four eyes symbolically represents four base pairs of the DNA base sequence. Which have genetic information about the deeds of a individual in its particular base sequence, when and where a particular code will operate, it depends on the circumstances. In this fashion the Vedic seers through their skill and wisdom have preserved their knowledge of the creation in the Vedic hymns. They have transferred their knowledge for the next succeeding generations, through oral recitation from generation to generation by using the laws of phonetics. Which is in it self a miracle that the knowledge of the vedic culture has reached to us even after many thousands years, through the vedic hymns in their original unbroken sequence.

Looking to the depth of knowledge in the vedic hymns, it proves that the vedic culture had reached at its top of development, through their skill of work on the earth. If we say that such type of development is not possible and the knowledge of the veda is beyond imagination than it will be sufficient to prove them as *Aporuṣeya.* It depends on the person concerns that how they digest the knowledge of the vedic hymns.

For the scholars and scientists a scientific Index to the Vedic deities has been given in the book for interpretation of the Vedic hymns, I have used the translations and commentaries as given by Griffith, Whitney, Wilson, Max Muller, A. A. Macdonell and commentary of Sāyaṇāchārya on the Vedic hymns. I hope that it will give a guideline for the interpretation in its proper way but the circumstances. and the context in which reference the hymn is, it will be more important. I bow to the Vedic seers and feel obliged to all, who have given me supports in different ways. Fellowsip by the department of Culture and financial assistance by UGC, New Delhi have supported me fully.

Specially, I am thankful to my Prof. L.P. Mall, Prof. R.R. Das, Prof. S.S. Nigam for guidance and Prof. V.N. Jha and Shri Chetanya kumar Jhalani for encouragement.

I feel great honour and obligation of Dr. Balram Jakhar, Governor of Madhya Pradesh for writing the Foreword of the book.

11-5-2005

C.P.Trivedi

Ratlam

Dedicated to the people of Indian Sub-continent

Dr. C.P. Trivedi

Part I
Introduction

1
Introduction

a. Early History

The Vedas are oldest literary record of human civilization on the earth, my traditional family back ground of *the Vedic* Culture and knowledge of ecology has given me deep insight in to the Vedas. In this reference it is import ant to note that it was only in 326 B.C. When Alexander the great made his raid in to the north western provinces of the subcontinent, with this the world came to know about the India and the Indian Culture, other major events in the History of India was the discovery of ancient cities of the Indus civilization and excavation at *Harappa* and *Mohenjo-daro* in the 1920s. With this the great history of the Indian Culture came in to Light, accordingly the Archeologists and Historians like Sir John Marshall, Sir William Jones who was a noted Scholar and Jurist of Calcutta High Court in 1786. They have worked on Indian culture and postulated that the Sanskrit language is more close to Latin, Greek and the languages of north India, with this Sir William Jones has established the fact that the languages of South India are distantly different from the Sanskrit and divided the Indians into the Āryan and non-Āryan. Rev. Robert Caldwell 1814 had used the term Dravidian for the people of South India. Accordingly they have propounded the hypothesis that the Aryans came in to India from the out side and inhabited the area of the Punjab and so on. Besides the British rulers of India have forced the Indians to think in the language of the Religion that religiously either they are Hindu or Muslim, although the term Hindu was derived from Hindustan and was synonym to the Indian.

Their motto was to explore the Indian culture but became also a diplomacy to create rifts between the different sects of the Indians, so that unanimously a revolution against the British Empire may not be there in India, along with this the supremacy of the European culture was there in their mind and as such a series of monumental work came out on *Race, Language and Culture*. There was much writing about *Āryans* Indo-European and the Harappan civilization and of its relationship to Egypt and especially Sumer, even Sir John Marshal has used the term "*Indo-Sumerian Civilization*" They have linked the history of India to the other early centers of the civilization in the light of the Biblical theory of creation.

Although the western scholars have done a great job for the Indian culture and history, but they were having their own limitations about the Indian culture. They have interpreted available records in their own way, with their western knowledge in the background. As such the theory of Aryan invasion and concept of Hindu Religion need a further investigation, which have created wrong notions about the Indian culture at a length. In this connection the knowledge of the vedic hymns can throw new light on the above concepts, which are integrated part of India and Indian culture as a whole.

The seeds of disintegration of India were sown without tracing the facts, and ultimately at the time of Independence, India was divided into the India and Pakistan on the name of the so called Religion, which has divided the Indians also, which is the main cause of unrest in the Indian subcontinent.

Study of the Vedas in the light of modern science reveals the fact that theory of Āryan invasion from outside India has no firm background.

b. The Vedic Literature

Vedas are the earliest text in the history of human civilization on the earth. Literary *Veda* means knowledge, which have the knowledge of the creation. There are four

Vedas: Ṛgveda, Yajurveda, Sāmaveda and Atharvaveda. Ṛgveda is the earliest and most of the hymns of the Ṛgveda are found in other Veda also, originally only three Vedas have been recognized, the knowledge there in is known as *Trayī Vidyā*. Rgveda is the book of *Praise, Sāmaveda* is the book of chants and *Yajurveda* supply the sacrificial formula for the sacrifice. *Atharva-veda* get included later on in the series, it deals with the some of the faiths of common people and medicines. It seems that *Atharvaveda* has been least understood, it has cosmological hymns also, which reveals the scientific knowledge of the creation.

After the *Vedic* period the Vedic knowledge became traditional, as such the formulas of *sacrfiicial* ceremony became traditional. To preserve the knowledge of *the Vedic hymns* and *Yajna* processes, *the Brāhmaṇa* literature came in to existence, every *Veda* has its related *Brāhmaṇa*, it has three parts- first part is *Brāhmaṇa*, second part is *Aranyak* and third part is *Upanishad. The Brāhmaṇas* are related with the sacrifice *Aranyak* are for deep thinking in the forest and *Upanishad are* related with the philosophical thoughts.

The Brāhmaṇa literature is under the category of *Shruti*, which was heard directly, but they are not *Veda. The Brāhmaṇa literature* contains a detailed knowledge of the sacrifice and sacrificial ceremonies in detail, which are very complicated, hence during the *Brahmana Period*, the systematic knowledge of the sacrificial ceremonies and formulas in short have been incorporated in the *Sutra Sahitya*. This literature is known as *Smṛti*, as the traditions are being preserved through remembering the processes. The same literature is known as *Kalp sutra*. There are different *Kalpa* Sutras, -

1. *Śhrauta Śūtra* which have systematic knowledge of the sacrificial ceremony.
2. *Grahya Śūtra* which has knowledge of the traditions, related with the family life.
3. *Dharma Śūtra* which have the knowledge of the duties related with the four *Varna* and four stages of life.

4. *Shulva Śūtra*, which have the knowledge for the preparation of *Yajna vedi* .It is related with the Geometry.

With this long history of *the Vedic* literature, Vedic hymns are symbolic having the knowledge in the form of metaphors and riddles; hence without the full knowledge of the creation and the different branches of *Veda,* it is difficult to interpret the meanings of the vedic hymns. With the development of modern science and technology, up to some extent we have touched the height of the vedic civilization, hence in the light of the modern knowledge it is possible to interpret the *Vedic hymns* up to some extent. Besides, there are *Vedanga* as *Āyurveda, Dhanurveda, Gandharvaveda* and *Jyortirveda.* The vedic knowledge can't be understood without the knowledge of *1. Shikshā 2. Nirukta 3. Vyākaraṇa 4. Chhanda 5. Jyotiṣa 6. Kalpa.*

The most important work on *the Veda* is the commentary of *Sāyaṇāchārya* on which most of the translations are based. *Yask* holds a prominent position among commentators. He has given his commentary in *Nirukta*, he has used *Nighantu* for explanation of the words.

Ṛgvedic deities have been described in *the Sarvānukramaṇi* of *Kātyāyana, which* is an index to the *Ṛgvedic mantras. Nītimañjarī* another commentary provides a idea about the social customs and tendencies of *the Ṛgvedic* period.

Different commentaries on the *Veda* can help in the interpretation of *the vedic* knowledge.

c. Age of the Vedas

As regard the age of the Vedas and Vedic culture is concern, it has been regarded that the vedic hymns were formulated around 2000 to 4000 years B.C. The archaeologists, historians and astronomers have different views regarding the age of the vedic hymns and they have no consensus over it. Looking to the depth of the vedic knowledge in the light of modern science, it seems that the vedic culture may have flourished on the earth before the ice age. The Green House Effect with consequent Global warming had forced them to compile their knowledge in the vedic hymns. As per the Hamburg Institute of Meteorology of Max Planck Society, Germany, under a project on *Climap* has reported that identical to today's "Green house Effect" and consequent Global warming had occurred about 18000 years ago and a consequent ice age was there. With this North America, Europe and Siberia were covered with the thick snow cover, in between Siberia and Alaska a land bridge was formed through which people were migrated. (German News Sept. 89, Page 25).It indicates that Vedic hymns may have been formulated at least about 18 thousand years ago.

2
The Natural Components as Deities

The natural components have been invoked as the deities, nuture has been invoked as goddess Aditi.

Aditi is the mother of a small group of Gods known as *Ādityas*, of whom *Varuṇa* is the chief. In the cosmogonic hymn *Dakṣa* is said to have sprung from *Aditi* and *Aditi* from *Dakṣa* (Rg. 10-72-4), this reciprocal relationship indicates that in the primeval condition of the creation, the fundamental charged particles constitutes the micro nature from which *Dakṣa* the solar nebula came in to existence from the nebula the solar system and the nature came in to existence.

Aditi's eight sons represents eight planets of the solar system. *Vasus* are related with the natural forces through which nature is working.

Aditi is associated with all the natural components. The natural components have been described as deities and have been invoked as God, which give a different look on these deities. But if we concentrate with deep insight on these natural deities than their connection with functions of the nature gets almost clear. There are about thirty three gods as described in the Ṛgveda, which can be grouped in to three, belonging to the three divisions of the universe earth, atmosphere and the sky.

Terrestrial deities are earth, *Agni* and *Soma*.

Atmospheric deities are *Indra*, *Apam Napat, Rudra, Maruts*,-Air, *Parjanya* and *Apas*-the waters.

Deities of the sky are *Dyaus*, sun and the solar phenomena related with the sun-such as *Varuna, Mitra, Savitra, Pushan*, the *Aswins* and the Goddesses *Usas, Dawn* and *Ratri*–night.

Physical features of the Vedic deities are anthropomorphic. Thus head, face eyes, arms, hands, feet and other portions of the human frame as ascribed to them are symbolic. The figurative description is simply meant to describe their activities figuratively, otherwise their connection with nature and natural phenomena are almost clear. It is also evident from the fact that there is no description of idols and temples in the Rigveda. It means the figures are symbolic expressions of their activities, which can be easily understood if concern knowledge is there.

The deities have a beginning and are not thought to born erroniously at the same time, sometimes the vedic seers have referred the earlier deities and certain deities have been described as the offsprings of others, which indicates that the natural forces have been generated from one another. The Deities became immortal by drinking soma is a symbolic expression of a chemical phenomena, which initiates the formation of the atoms and molecules of the natural components, where *Soma* is a bond energy, which bind atoms and provide them stability. The offsprings of the deities signifies that the natural components and forces are interconnected and one force may generate the other.The home of the deities have been described as sky (heavan), which indicates sun and zone of ionosphere in the upper atmosphere. Each deity has been considered as supreme and mighty, which regulates the order of nature no one can thwart their ordinance, it means that natural components are independent in themselves and inevitable for the nature.

About a dozen deities have been invoked in pairs such as *Dyava–prthivi* 'heavan and earth' *Mitra–Varuna, Āpam Napat, Agni–Soma* and *Indra–Soma.*

Besides the pair of deities, there are a certain number of more or less definite groups of deities. They are associated with some particular God, such as *maruts-* storm gods, *Rudras* have been associated with their father *Rudra* and *Ādityas* have been mentioned in company with their mother *Aditi*. Another important group is of *Vasus*. *Indra* has been associated with *Indras.* There are also *Visve devas* means all Gods.

Invoking the deities in pairs and in groups. It indicates their connections with each other, which signifies that for their functions in the nature they are dependent and associated with each other, although independently they are supreme and inevitable for the functions of the nature.

The deities have been described as great, they regulates the order of the nature, they hold sway over all creatures, one can by pass their ordinance through invoking them. Fulfillment of the desires depends on them, they bestow prosperity to the mankind; only one in whom injurious traits appear is *Rudra.*

Natural deities are true and have been regarded as friends and protector of the honest. They punish sin and guilt. It means that the natural benefactors are for wise utilization, whenever over exploitation is there, or misuse of the natural components is there, consequent imbalance in the nature may be the cause of natural catastrophe, the same is the punishment for the mankind.

a. Deities of the Sky

Deities of the Sky are *Dyauṣ–Varuṇa, Mitra, Śurya, Savitra, Pūṣan,* the *Āswins, Uṣas* and *Rātrī.* They represents solar phenomena. Sun has been regarded as the main energy source on the earth and has been described as the eye and the soul of the creation. All the activities, which are going on in the creation have been attributed to the sun.

Kāla-time Atharvaveda 19-53,54, is the main cause of the creation, the time is responsible for everything. The time is get calculated with sun's movement at its axis, which is known as *the Samvatsara Kāla* or year. Alongwith this all the planets in the solar system are moving around the sun and rotate at their axis, through their magnetic field, they influence weather and climate on the earth's surface. The duration of the day and night with rising and setting of the sun are related with the solar phenomena. The germinating plants shows maximum growth during the morning and evening hours. Hence the morning and evening have been regarded as auspicious time for the health purpose, Vedic seers have drawn the attention towards the same, The *Aswin* represents morning and evening, The savitra is the stimulator of metabolic reactions in the living beings. *Aswins* are the sign of longevity, it means if the morning and evening hours are utilized properly, they can check aging. *Mitra* is the visible light of the sun, which is essential for photosynthesis and important for the creation, as such *Mitra*-light is friend of all the creatures. *Mitra* has been invoked with *Varuṇa, and the Varuṇa* is God of water, it means with the visibility of light, temperature get increases, which initiates evoporation and transpirantion, which are responsible for the rainfall. *Matriswan*, which is said to produce in the heaven and has been brought on the earth, it indicates that the carbon get generated in the heaven and its next birth is on the earth, where it get produced during the oxidation as carbon di oxide.

b. Deities of the Atmosphere

Atmospheric deities are *Indra Āpam-napat, Rudra*, the *maruts, Vāyu, Parjanya and Āpas*-the waters.

Indra has been described as the lord of the atmospheric deities, he is regarded as twin brother of *Agni*, his physical features are anthropomorphic, his arms and the weapons are the indicators of the atmospheric activities. *Indra* has close connection with *Soma, Varuna, Sun and Aditi*, it signifies its universal nature.

In actual sense *Indra* represents electric energy. In the Veda *Soma* has been described as a plant, as a moon and as an energy also, he is the lord of speech, plants, earth, sun and moon. It means, he is associated with them and as such they have been identified as *Soma*, which signifies magnetic energy within them. *Soma* and *Indra* together represents electromagnetic energy. As such *Indra* and *Soma* are the essential part of nature *(Aditi)*. *Varuna* has been identified as lord of water, water consist of H_2O-hydrogen and oxygen.

The bond energy-electromagnetic energy in the water molecule has been indicated through *Soma* and *Indra.*

The atmospheric activities lightning, rainfall, thunder storm and wind flow are associated with the electricity. Today it is a fact that atmospheric layers-troposphere, mesosphere, stratosphere, ionosphere and the magnetosphere are interconnected through global electric circuit G E C and are influenced by each other. The activities of these layers, ultimately affects weather and climate on the earth. Symbolically the same has been indicated through the activity of *the Indra*, his thunder bolt *Vajra* is his electric charge, his drink *Soma* is a magnetic energy. When the electrical and magnetic disturbances are there in the atmosphere, then the electricity with the disturbed magnetic field brings magnetic storms and thunder storms, which creates havoc in the atmosphere and on the earth. The same has been described as energetic angry nature of *the Indra*. The *Soma* has been described as *Āpam napat*, which bring rains, *Parjanya* are rain clouds, which are having positive & negative charges. When these two charges colloids it causes lightning and rain, the same has been described as killing of the demon of draught-*Vṛtra* by *the Indra*. The battle of *Indra* with *Vṛtra* to release the imprisoned cow is a symbolic expression for the rainfall, as rains have been described as milk, ghee or honey, which signifies the nourishing character of the rainwater and cow is a metaphor for the rain clouds.

Maruts have been described with *Indra, Rudra* and *Vayu*-wind, they are related with the clouds in the atmosphere. Which check the sun light, their father is *Rudra*, there are eleven *Rudra*, which have been described with air, which signifies oxygen. When it is said that *Rudra* is having medicinal properties, he is physician of physicians. It means with oxygen he provides remedies for the diseases, which is its beneficial aspect or *Siva Bhava*, till the capacity of breathing is there in the living beings, they survive. When respiration get seized, the same oxygen oxidise the dead, which is its meleficent demon like character. *Rudra* initiates oxidation-reduction reactions in the atmosphere, hence he is regarded as their father, the *Indra*–electricity and wind, when they colloid in the atmosphere, they produce thunder storm, roaring, lightning and rainfall. Hence the *Maruts* have been described with *the Indra*. With the rain fall clouds became disappear and the sunlight is visible. Sun has been personified as *Vishnu* Rig. 1-154. *Vishnu* is the visible form of light on the earth, which gets associated with all the biological and chemical reactions going on in the nature. His three steps are sky, *Antriksha* and the earth, which is a course of light from the sun to the earth. It has been said that his two steps are visible and one step is invisible, it means in the *Antariksha*, where the ozone layer absorbs the UV radiations. It is his invisible step, the other two steps represents sun in the sky and the visible light on the earth's surface. Different forms of the water have been invoked as *Apas* and *Apam-napat* (Rigveda 2-35). The water has been identified as *Agni* and as sun of water, which represents water vapours, the *Agni garbha*–embrys of water, it indicates about the electromagnetic bond energy, which binds hydrogen and oxygen atoms in a water molecule.

c. The Terrestrial Deities

Terrestrial deities are *Pṛthvi–Earth, Agni* and *Soma.*

Pṛthvi–Earth has been invoked as the dwelling place for natural components. It provides space for the nature and natural activities. Agni is the main source of energy on the earth. Agni has three birthplaces with three fold nature. The three birth places are sky, *Antavriksha* and earth. The sky is the place of sun, where it has its first birth, from there it came to *Antavriksha*, where it is trapped by the earth's magnetosphere. Where magnetospheric processes have given it a second birth, from here it came on the earth's surface, where plants convert the visible light in to the chemical energy. It is its third birth. The actions and inter-actions going on at these three places have given it a threefold nature. *Agni* - energy is the cause of creation, it has been indicated in the very first stanza of the Rigveda—1-1-1.

अग्निमीळे पुरोहितं यज्ञस्य देवमृत्विजम्। होतारं रत्नधातमम्॥ १॥

I call *Agni*-energy, which is priest, deity and (Rtvij) the invoker of the sacrifice, the bestower of treasure.

Here sacrifice signifies the creation sacrifice-actions and inter-actions, which are going on in the creation, through which creation has its beginning and a source of its existence.

The Soma is a terrestrial deity, on the earth it represents geomagnetic field of the earth. The Soma is associated with *Indra, Agni, Pusan* and *Rudra*. *The Soma* is a companion of *Indra* and they ride on the same car, it indicates that *Indra* is electricity and *Soma* is a magnetic energy, which together known as electromagnetic energy, accordingly they have been invoked with each other as riding on the same car.

सोमेनादित्या बलिनः सोमेन पृथिवी मही।

अथो नक्षत्राणामेषामुपस्थे सोम आहितः॥ ऋ. 10-85-2

By *Soma* are the *Adityas* strong, by *Soma* mighty is the earth.

This *Soma* in the midst of all these constellations hath his place.

In fact *Soma* signifies magnetic energy, power of the sun is in *Soma* means its magnetic spots and magnetic field, the earth is great due to the *Soma* means earth's geomagnetic field and magnetosphere. In other as in *Nakṣhtrāṇi* (astronomical bodies) *Soma* is present. It indicates that the magnetism is present in all the astronomical bodies. According to the modern astronomical principles every rotating astronomical body, which is moving at its axis is having its own magnetic field and magnetosphere.

A plant growing on mountains is also known as *Soma* plant, which is used in preparation of *Soma* juice. It is due to the power of stimulation in it, otherwise all plants are having *Soma*. In some hymns of Atharvaveda and in post Vedic era the moon has been identified as *Soma*, it signifies the magnetic power of the moon. The moon is a planet of the earth and having induced magnetic field, which influence the earth's geomagnetic field and life processes on the earth, it influences nervous system of the living beings through brain, the lunatic persons behave abnormally during full moon or dark night, due to this stimulating power of moon, the moon has been termed as *Soma* and it is said that in the human body mind is like a moon.

3

Scientific Index to the Vedic Hymns

Vedic deities are the source to understand the vedic hymns. The deities, signifies either a component of nature or natural phenomena, which they represent. With a long history of the vedic culture, which may be about many thousands of years, the names of the vedic deities get transformed in to the personification and worship of nature and natural phenomena, which have been became converted in to the belief that all the objects and the nature with which man is surrounded are animate and divine. Accordingly with time the vedic deities were being interpreted in different ways according to the fancy of the narrator. As the stories related with the deities have been described in the anthropomorphic manner, the natural basis of the deity get lost and the anthropomorphic nature of the vedic deities has given the way for personification of the deities and description of the vedic deities as if they have offsprings and generations. The same has given the concept that Vedic Gods have families. Heaven and earth are the parent of the vedic Gods, accordingly the description of the vedic deities have taken the shape of myths. Hence in the present era the names of the vedic deities are having a altogether different meanings. Otherwise the names of the vedic deities originally represents different forces and components of the nature. As has been revealed from the fact that the vedic culture was having the full knowledge of the creation and before the catastrophe, which was inevitable under natural circumstances, the vedic seers have compiled their knowledge of the creation in the vedic hymns. The vedic metaphors are having the indication of the natural phenomena or a chemical reaction. The language of the vedic hymns is coded and symbolic. The deities and the meanings of the words are only to indicate the related phenomena or reaction. Which have been described metaphorically under a family or agroups of deities. The figurative description of the deities is only to indicate their activities figuratively.

Every individual deity is independent and supreme as a head of the family, it means that the deity is inevitable for function of the nature and the inter relationship of the various factors is responsible for a particular phenomena of nature, it has been indicated through the agency of its family of the vedic deities, which are interrelated for a function. The interrelationship of various factors have been shown through offsprings, brother, sister, spouse, mother and father etc. This interrelationship can be understood if we are acquainted with the scientific terminology of the vedic deities, as names of the vedic deities represents the natural forces and natural factors, and their relation with other forces, which are working in the nature.

The functions of the Vedic deities have been expressed in an anthropomorphic manner to indicate the physical phenomena, which they represents. Thus the ancient commentator on Veda *Yaska* (Nir. 7, 4) speaking on the nature of Gods, remarks that what is seen of them is not anthropomorphic at all, as in the case of the sun, the earth and others. Hence the way through which the vedic seers have expressed their knowledge is personification of the deities, by which the natural phenomena is being indicated figuratively. After the destruction of the vedic culture the natural phenomena and deities became modified in to the worship of Gods.

Invoking the natural deities is a peculiar feature of the vedic culture, which signifies that every thing, object or a natural phenomena with which we are surrounded are having a good or evil influence on us, as such, heaven, earth, mountains, rivers, plants, animals, and even objects made by hand such as weapons, chariot, music drums, plough, pressing stones, sacrificial post have been invoked. It is only to indicate that every thing, which is present in the nature. They have their own importance and are for wise utilization, as the vedic seers have invoked the *manyu*-wrath and *shriddha*-respect also. It was having the motto that every one should feel sense of responsibility towards the nature and its conservation

The basic forces of the nature are true Gods of Veda, which can be inspired with motives and have passion born like man, but immortal. In fact they are representatives of the phenomena of nature. The degree of anthropomorphism of the various deities varies considerably because when the name of the God is the same as that of his natural function than the personification is not advanced, such is the case with *dyau*-sky, heaven-middle atmosphere, *Pṛthvi*-earth, *surya*-sun, *usha*-dawn, whose names represent the double character of the natural phenomena and of the force presiding over them. Due to which they have their existence.

The *Vedic* deities have but very few indistinguishing features, while many attributes and powers are shared by all alike. This is partly due to the fact that the department of nature, which they indicates are often much in common. The deities have common source but have different forms to denote a particular phenomena, which gradually has acquired an independent character.

It means the forces of the nature are having a common source and are interrelated. For the phenomena of nature one particular force is responsible, which is independent in it self and inevitable for the nature.

Today it is a fact that on the earth whatever is going on is due to the sun, which influence, weather, climate and life on the earth through its various natural forces. The same has been described as "The sun is the soul and eye of the creation"

The Universe, which is the stage on which the actions of Vedic deities are going on has been regarded as three fold, which may be divided in to three domains of earth, atmosphere and heaven. Accordingly the vedic deities have been classified, which are mainly thirtythree in number and can be divided equally eleven in each sphere. In the *Brāhmaṇa* literature they are classified as eight terrestrial *Vasus*, aeriel eleven *Rudra* and celestial twelve *Āditya*. Which are related with earth, wind and sun respectively, *Sarvanukramni of kātyāyana* deals with Vedic deities in detail, which is a index to Vedic deities. Following the triple classification of Ṛgveda 1-139 *Yask* (*Ṇīr.*7, 5) has divided the different deities in the fifth chapter of *Naighaṇṭuka* in to the three orders of *Pṛthvi sthāna*-terrestrial (*Ṇīr.*7, 14-9.43) *Antarikṣa sthāna* aerial (*Ṇir.*10, 1-11.50) and *Dyau sthāna*-celestral (12, 1-46) He further explain that in the opinion of his predecessors *Nairuktah* there are only three main deities, these are *Agni* on earth, *Vayu* in air and *Surya*-sun in heaven. It indicates about the importance of three main spheres of the world as reflected in Rg. 10-158 May *Surya* protect us from heaven, *Vat* from air and *Agni* from the earthly regions.

The fifth chapter of *Naighantuka*, on which *Yask* comments contains in its enumeration of Gods a number of minor deities also so that the number of deities in different spheres became more than eleven. It is important to note that in this list of Gods prthivi and *Tvastar* are common in all spheres, some Gods are common in terrestrial as well as aerial, such as *Agni* and *Usha*, *Varuṇa*, *Yama Savitra* in the aerial as well a in the celestial. In this manner the classification is according to the relative importance of the deities in different spheres. Which indicates that the natural factors, equally influence other spheres also through their actions.

The description of Gods-deities metaphorically as a warrior, or as a moral ruler and accordingly the glorification of the deities enumerate them as super natural powers. This has given the way for mythological interpretations of the deities after the vedic period. If we concentrate on the relative importance of the vedic deities other than super natural powers, then only we can interpret the names of Vedic deities.

Scientific interpretation of the vedic terminology is not to glorify the vedic culture but for the guidance of the modern scientists, who can take the guidelines from the phenomena or reaction so as to work on the untouched aspects of the creation system.

Vedic terminology starting from the Rigveda with time have taken different turn, they have been explained in *Atharvaveda* also. In *Brāhamaṇa*, *Upanishads* and *Purāṇas* they have taken a totally different turn being associated with spiritual experiences and their imagination in the form of personified super natural powers. Which has given the way for narration of the myths in different shapes and forms, which became the basis of Indian mythology as we know today.

Association of Vedic terminology with myths of mythology, which is a product of long history of time and climatic conditions. Along with this due to the coded language of the vedic hymns, the subject matter is complex and difficult to interpret. Once the key of metaphors is with us than we can interpret the natural phenomena as indicated by the vedic hymns, with the help of modern knowledge. Which can give a new field of research and the riddles given in the vedic hymns can be solved.

The whole creation is a family under the fundamental energy, from where the creation came into existence. The creation is working as a system, through transformation of energy with actions and interactions in cyclic manners (Rg. 10-90-16). The earth, where life is present, it also represents a family, where sky is father, earth is mother *soma*- magnetic energy is brother, *Aditi*-nature is sister (Rg. 10-191-6), accordingly every natural force and its related phenomena have been described as different families.

4

Scientific Index to the Vedic Deities

Aditi ....Infinite nature, micro nature

Aditi ....Nature (The name cow is used for nature, due to its nourishing capacity

Āditya ....Twelve Aditya (twelve months)

Agni ....Fire, energy

Aja ....Unborn, Aja means goat also

Āpah ....Water

Āpam napat ....Son's of water-steam

Apsarā ....Chemical reaction, which are going on in a cyclic manner

Aryamā ....A ray of sun, long red wave length of light

Aśva ....Horse-a form of rapidly moving energy

Asvattha ....Ficus religiosa, pipal

Āswin ....Morning and evening, they represents a pair, union of two, they are twin sons of Vivasvat-nucleotide pair, represents rising and settng of sun

Audumbar ....Ficus glumerata-fig

Avi ....Protector of plant, sheep

Bhāga ....Amsa, a portion

Bhṛgu ....Shining, chlorophyll

Chamsam .... Chalice,cup-cell, Parna Mani, Chlorophyll

Dakṣa .... Condensed form of energy, which has produced nebula

Darbha .... Grass

Dasagavs .... Ten, ten rays

Deva .... Fundamental particles, God

Devatā .... Natural forces

Dharma .... Work, duty

Dhenu .... Cow

Eagle .... Sun rays

Gandharva .... Water nymph, protoplasm

Garutmāna, Suparṇa .. Brilliant luster of sun rays (sun bird)

Gāyatri .... Three bands o fundamental particles. (electron, proton, neutron, energy)

Ghṛta-butter .... Condensed form of energy

Ghṛta prasṭha .... Condensed energy in organic matter

Gladdening Drop .... Life energy

Havi .... Stimulator

Idā-Iḷā .... Nourishment

Indra .... Bolt of Indra, The electrical charge

Indra .... Electricity, -two steeds-two charges +ive & -ive

Kutsa .... Sun spots.

Mahī-bhāratī .... The great earth

Mārṭaṇḍa .... Earth, Āditya

Maruts .... Storm, thunder

Mātariśvā .... CO_2 carbon dioxide (crippled cow)

Mitra .... Light, friend

Mother .... Symbol of progeny and nourishment

Narsams ....A particular ray of sun, short blue wave length of light

Navagvas ....Nine, The nine doors of the human body

Nave ....Center

Nigrodha ....Ficus bengalensis-banyan

Nila-lohita ....Blue and red rays of sun

Pañcha Jana ....Five types of living beings

Parjanya ....Rain clouds, due to the nourishing capacity of rains, they have been called as cow and the rain water as milk

Parṇa maṇi ....Chlorophyll

Pavamāna ....O_2 oxygen

Pegs ....Cycles

Pishācha ....Rakshas-flesh eater microbes

Pishanga......................Toxic rays

Prajāpati ....Lord of beings (fundamental energy)

Puruṣa ....Symbolic imagination of fundamental, energy

Purohita ....Priest

Pūṣan ....Nourishment, solar rays

Ṛta ....Cosmic principle

Rudra Āgni ....Energy in the gaseous air

Rudra Soma ....Magnetic energy, which bind the nuclear particle in atoms of gaseous air

Sādhya ....Material

Samidhā ....Fuel

Sarasvatī ....Vac, speech, a river

Savitra ....Stimulator

Seven Aditya .... Seven sons of Aditi—seven planets

Sinivalī .... Duplicating DNA, Which initiate language code in DNA

Soma .... Magnetic energy, forces and formation of bond energy, drinking of soma-association of magnetic energy with others, such as-Indra & soma electromagnetic energy

Somagopa .... Guardian of soma, soma is also a name of a plant as well as moon due to the presence of magnetic energy (soma)

Sudhanvā .... Son of Sudhanvan, developing cell, Ṛbhu

Sūrya .... Sun

Svarbhanu .... Eclipse of Sun-Rahu

Tanunāpata .... Solar flares

Ten fingers .... Ten, ten rays

Triśīra .... Triplet code

Trit .... Three, triple bond Ḥ3 who prepare soma

Tvastā .... DNA

Uṣā .... Dawn

Vāchaspati .... Lord of speech

Vaja .... Younger, (vigorous one)

Varuṇa .... Gravity, gravitational force, as soon as atoms and molecules are get formed they have their existence the same has been described as Varuṇa who is the lord of water means the water molecules are having the cohesive force

Varuṇa Soma .... The magnetic energy of the atoms, molecules and substances

Vibhvan .... Eminent

Viṣṇu .... Course of solar rays from sky, heaven and atmosphere, its two steps are visible but its one step is invisible means absorption of ultraviolet rays in the upper atmosphere by ozone layer, which is its invisible step

Viśvakarmā .... Creator, carpentor (fundamental Energy)

Viśvarūpa .... Son of Tvastra, who is responsible for various forms of living beings

Vivasvata .... Vivasvat's son manu called as vaivasvata or yama-yami, DNA

Wheel .... Cycle, chakra

Yajna .... Sacrifice, actions and interactions

Yajnayavedi .... Place of reaction

Yāma .... Chromosome, with information of life and death

Yama-Yamī .... The twin brother and sister, they represents a pair of chromosomes

Yuj .... To connect

5
The Vedic Concept of Biosphere

a. Ecosystem

Ecology is a science, which investigates organisms in relation to their environment and a philosophy in which the world of life is being interpreted in terms of natural processes. Recent developments in the field of ecology has recognised that natural components biotic and abiotic are inter related and they function in an orderly manner as a definite system. The same is known as ecosystem, as such the whole world is a ecosystem, which develop gradually and reach at its peak through actions and interactions in a cyclic manner in the nature. The stability of an ecosystem lies in the equilibriun of its different components, which is being maintained through homeostasis and ecological check and balance, known as the science of cybernetics. In this way an ecosystem is a selfsufficient and self regulated unit.

The nature is also an ecosystem, where main energy source is the sun as a part of the nature. The earth which have biotic and abiotic components is known as biosphere with complex processes within it. Through weather and climate it influences life on the earth in multi directional ways. With the time whenever a imbalance is there in between its components under natural circumstances, the ecosystem under go degradation and finally collapsed if not checked properly.

The stability of an ecosystem depends on the equilibrium in between its components, at the same time there must be a balance between producer plants and consumer animals. the plants are the primary producers, they synthesise food material for the creation at primary level through photosynthesis. As well as they produce oxygen which is essential for life, besides the plants are the only source, which convert light energy in to the chemical energy on the earth, it means the ecosystem is directly influenced by its plant population.

Now it is a scientific fact that life on the earth is purely a natural process of evolution. Life on the earth is due to the presence of ozone layer in the upper atmosphere, which acts as a shield against toxic ultraviolet rays, it absorbs them and filters all the radiations below 3000 Ñ. Thus ozone layer is directly related with life sustaining processess on the earth. Similarly earth's magnetic field and magnetosphere protects the earth from high energetic solar wind.

The nature is self sufficient and self regulated but external influences and human disturbences may cause imbalance. At present the earth is facing the same situation, due to the rapid industrialization, population explosion and the deforestation at global level. It is the cause of global warming through 'green house effect'. The depletion of ozone layer due to the pollutants like chloro fluoro carbon, nitrogen oxide and hydrocarbons. It has produced a serious threat to the life on the earth.

According to the Hamburg Institute for Meteorology of Max Plank Society, indentical to today's 'green house effect' and consequent global warming had occured about 18000 years ago (German news Sept. 89 page 25) and a ice age was there, it means earth has faced similar situation earlier too, the same we are facing today.

b. The Vedic Culture

Once in the history of the earth *Vedic* culture was all over the world, which spread with time and established a harmonious equilibrium with nature, as they were having full knowledge of the creation. Which is similar to our present day knowledge of the creation and life on the earth. Under natural circumstances the *Vedic* culture was get ruined due to the natural catastrophe like earth quake and volcano eruptions. Before the catastrophe they may have faced the problem of global warming, as indicated in *the Vedic hymns.* A. 10-8. 39, 40

The Vedic culture was developed in different fields of knowledge, accordingly they have described the origin and evolution of the creation in a scientific manner. They have revealed the fact that the origin and evolution of the creation is purely a natural phenomena, which came into existence from an fundamental energy, through actions and interactions in the cyclic manners Ath. 10-7-42, 43, 44. For the creation *Kāla*-time is important. Ath. 8. 8-23, Rg. 1-164-48. They have described the fundamental energy under the name of *Visvakarma, Prajāpati and Puruṣa.*

The Vedic *Yajna* is a symbolic representation of actions and inter actions going on in the nature in a cyclic manner Rg. 1.164-50 & Rg. 10-90-16. Accordingly the whole creation is a *Srishti Yagnya*, which came in to existence through the actions and inter actions under a system. The Vedic seers have indicated it in the first hymn of Rg. 1-1-1

I invoke the *Agni*-(fundamental energy) who is the *Deva* (fundamental particles), sacrificer, and reciter of the *Sristi, Yajna*, which is the treasure of jewels.

It means every thing, which is present in the creation is due to the fundamental energy.

The Vedic seers have described the nature with the name of *Aditi* and have postulated the fact that in this world what is and what is to be is nature only.

Aditi is the heaven, *Aditi* is mid air, *Aditi* is the mother the Sire and Son: *Aditi* is all Gods, *Aditi* five-classed men, *Aditi* all that hath been born and shall be born. Rg. 1-89-10.

It indicates that every thing, which is going on in the creation is due to the *Aditi* (nature) as such the whole earth is one family. Rg. 1-191-6.

Heaven is your Sire, your Mother Earth, Soma your brother, *Aditi* your Sister: seeing all unseen, keep still and dwell ye happily.

The whole earth is one family is synonym to the modern concept of Biosphere.

c. The Vedic Deities

Looking to the fact that origin and evolution of life on the earth is purely a natural process of evolution, which is being influenced by the forces working in the nature. They have concluded that every thing, which is present on the earth and in the future also it will be only nature. (Rg. 1.89.10) Accordingly they have emphasized to maintain harmony and equilibrium with nature. As all the natural components whether biotic or abiotic are equally important, independently each component is complete in it self and inevitable for the nature, as such they have given due importance to the every component of nature, as reflected in their concept of *Vasudhaiv Kutumbakam* the whole earth is one family and regarded the natural components as the deities. Physical features of the Vedic deities are anthropomorphic. Thus head, face eyes, arms, hands, feet and other portions of the human frame as ascribed to them are symbolic. The figurative description is simply meant to describe their activities figuratively, otherwise their connection with nature and natural phenomena are almost clear. It is also evident from the fact that there is no description of the idols and temples in the Rigveda. To invoke the natural deities is having a deep sense of obligations towards the natural benefactors, which are useful in daily life. As we find in the veda that they have also invoked mountains, plough, forest, plants have been invoked as divine powers with healing properties (Rg. 10.97), pressing stones- mortar and pastles used in the preparation of soma juice, (Rg. 1.28.5.6) music drums used in the battle fields, arms, arrows (Rg. 6.75) Besides *Manyu* wrath Rg. 10.83, 84 *Shriddha* (Rg. 10.151) *Anumati* favour and *Aramati* - devotion have been invoked. Which indicates that everything which is useful in daily life should be used properly.

On the contrary to this there are aerial foes of deities, these are called as *Asura* and *Das* or *Dasyu* known as demons. Lower class of the demons are goblins, which are enemies of men, commonly they are known as *Rakshas, Pishachas* corpse.These are actually the microbes and contaminators of the air and soil. They have been termed as flash eaters. These are actually microbial parasites causing diseases in the human beings.

To invoke the natural deities is having a dual purpose, first to indicate the functions of the nature and activity of the natural components. As well as to create environmental awareness among the common people that the natural components are for wise utilization. Exploitation of the nature is a sin, for this nature will punish in its own way by the natural catastrophe. Which are due to the imbalance get created by the mankind in the nature. It is only in the post Vedic era that invoking the natural deities get transformed into the traditional worship and it has taken a superstitious turn.

d. Life on the Earth

In modern terminology the whole world is an ecosystem, in a balanced ecosystem all the components have their own importance, which emphasize the conservation of biodiversity in the nature. For life on the earth the presence of ozone layer in the upper atmosphere and earth's magnetic field and magnetosphere are equally important. All these facts have been indicated in the vedic hymns.

By saying that the sun is the soul and eye of the creation Rg. 1.115.1 they have indicated about the importance of the sun. In the Athrvaveda 1.32, presence of ozone layer and magnetosphere have been indicated. The truth has been revealed in a anthropomorohic manner.

By saying that the reason due to which plants breathe is not on the earth and not in the sky, but its station is in the mid air (The same is the place of ozone layer in the atmosphere, which absorbs ultraviolet rays) In the last two verses they have drawn attention towards magnetosphere and magnetospheric processes, which feed the creation like a source of ocean through ionosphere, where ions are being generated from fundamental particles. It has been indicated that the planets of the solar system are covered with interplanetary magnetic field and their existence in the solar system depends on their magnetic field.

Now, ye people, take knowledge, he will speak a great mystery (? *Brahaman*); that is not on the earth, nor in the sky where by the plants breathe. Ath. 1.32.1.

In the atmosphere is the station of them, as of those sitting wearied; the station of this that exists (*bhuta*): that the pious know or they do not. Ath 1.32.2.

What the(two) quaking firmaments (*rodasi*) and the earth- fashioned out, that at present is always wet, like the streams of Ocean. Ath. 1.32.3

One hath covered all, this rests upon the other both to the heaven and to the all-possessing earth have I paid homage. Ath. 1.32.4.

One of them clothes him self in this earth; one encompassed the atmosphere; he of them who is disposer (*vidhartr*) gives the sky; some defend respectively all regions. Ath.X.8.36.

The one who clothes himself in this earth is earth's magnetic field and one who encompassed the atmosphere is earth's magnetosphere, who protects the earth from the magnetic field of sun and other planets. Ath. 10.8.36.

The same has been indicated in Rigveda, symbolically in *Asya Wamiya Sukta*.

He With *Jagati* the flood in heaven he established, and saw the sun in the *Rathantara Saman*.

Gayatri hath, they say, three bands for kindling: hence it excels in majesty and vigour.Rg. 1.164.25.

The *Jagati* is the place in the atmospheric ocean, where the high energetic solar winds are trapped by the earth's magnetosphere, (*Gayatri's* three bands are three fundamental particles) where the three fundamental particles- electron, proton and neutron are get converted in to the ions, hence it excels in majesty and vigour. Rg. 1.164.25.

"*Dyaus* (sky) is my father, my begetter; kinship is here. This great earth is my kin and mother.

Between the wide spread world halves is my birthplace: the father laid the Daughter's germ within it.

The truth about the life on the earth has been explained through the mouth of the life symbolically, that the sun in the sky is my father, who is the cause of life, earth is my mother, who nourish me and my birth place is in between the world halves, (where ozone layer absorbs the toxic ultra violet rays), Rg.1-164-33.

It indicates that after knowing the facts behind life on the earth, the vedic seers have incorporated them in the vedic hymns and emphasize to maintain harmony with the nature and the natural components

In the cosmogonic hymns of Athervaveda, the vedic seers have indicated about the global warming in the hymn 10-8-, where the fundamental energy has been described as Skambh- frame of the creation. Accordingly the questions have been raised regarding the sustainer and regulator of the creation. The fundamental energy has been described as supporter, regulator and sustainer of the creation, from whom the creation came in to the existence. He regulates the creation through oxidation and reduction reactions in the nature Ath. 10.7.42, 43, 44. As a golden embryo, he is omnipotent and omnipresent, he sustain heaven and earth, he stood in the midst of creation as Yaksha, all are set in him like the branches of a tree.

A great monster' (yaksa) in the midst of the creation (bhuvan) strode? (kranta) in penace on the back of the sea- in it are set (cri) whatever gods there are like the branches of a tree roundabpout the trunk. Ath. 10.7.38.

It has been indicated through the metaphor of a tree, that all the components of the nature have been evolved from a single energy, all are linked with him like the branches of a tree, he is in the middle of the creation, it signifies the omnipotent nature of the fundamental energy.

How the Skambh-fundamental energy sustains the creation, it has been indicated through the *Samvatsar Kāla* (year) Ath. 10.8.4, and six seasons, which through temperature pressure gradient participate with him Ath. 10.8.5. 'He is unaging, an immortal in the house of mortals', it means the existence of atoms and the life energy in the living beings are dependent on him, his another form is Avi (chlorophyll) through which the trees are green and garlanded Ath. 10.8.31. It means autotrophic nature of the plants has been indicated.

e. Global warming

Global warming is a modern threat for existence of life on the earth, it seems that the earth may have faced this situation earlier too as indicated in the Atharvaveda in a lucid manner Ath.10.8.

यदन्तरा द्यावापृथिवी अग्निरैत् प्रदहन् विश्वदाव्यः।

यत्रातिष्ठन्नेकपत्नीः परस्तात् क्वेवासीन्मातरिश्वा तदानीम्॥ अर्थववेद 10-8-39

As between heaven-and earth Agni went, burning on, all-consuming, where stood beyond they of one husband - where perchance was mataricvan then ?

अप्स्वासीन्मातरिश्वा प्रविष्टः प्रविष्टा देवाः सलिलान्यासन्।

बृहन हं तस्थौ रजसो विमानः पवमानो हरित॥ अर्थववेद 10-8-40

Mataricvan was entered into the waters; the gods were entered into the seas; great stood the traverser of space; the purifying one entered into the green ones.

The Vedic seers have drawn the picture of the global warming, it has been indicated that during the period when in between earth and heaven fire go on burning and consuming all, it means due to the global warming, earth and heaven will have no difference. Looking to this a question has been asked? If such a condition will be there, in that condition where will be the lord of heaven and earth (fundamental energy)? Where will be the Matariswan (CO_2)? It has been indicated here that the lord of heaven and earth (fundamental energy) will be in the mid of space and Matariswan will enter into the water, it means it will be in the dissolved condition, the natural forces will remain in the ocean of the sky, the purifying one will enter in to the green one. It suggests that air purifier (chlorophyll) will be in the dormant condition. As we know that during unfavourable conditions the prokaryotes can form the cyst, which can reproduce with the return of favourable conditions. As such after catastrophe the process of evolution will again start similarly as before, where the power of Gayatri fundamental particles-(electron, proton and neutron) play their role. The Gayatri has been described as immortal -Amrit.The seer who has the knowledge about the synthesis of the substances, he can explain about the unseen fundamental bond energy, which binds the atoms.

उत्तरेणेव गायत्रीममृतेऽधि वि चक्रमे।

साम्ना ये साम संविदुरजस्तद् ददृशे क्व ।। अथर्ववेद 10-8-41

Higher, as it were, than the *gayatri,* upon the immortal (*amṛita*) he strode out; they who knows completely chant with chant-where then was seen the unborn one (*aja*).

In this way Vedic seers have described about the origin, evolution and the functions of the creation in an orderly manner, in a similar fashion as revealed by the modern scientific facts. For us sun is the main source of energy, above it they have indicated towards a single fundamental energy, which is responsible for the creativity of the sun and the creation. Rg. 10.89.2

स सूर्यः पर्युरु वरांस्येन्द्रो ववृत्याद्रथ्येव चक्रा । ऋ. 10-89-2

He (force) drives the Sun and the planets like a wheel of a chariot.

Part II

The Creation

6
The Creation and the Creator

How the creation came in to existence? who is the creator? who is the regulator? who is the supporter, protector and leader of the creation? All these questions have been discussed at a length in the Veda.

a. Modern Concept of Energy

The whole universe is filled with energy, there is only energy, at some places energy get condensed in as electrons, protons and neutrons, which bind together to produce atoms, and atoms in turn bound in to the molecules that produce substances, to whom we can touch, feel and call it as mass energy. In Einstein's equation $E=mc^2$ means energy and mass are interconvertible.

Our universe is a vast ocean of energy, where energy under goes transformation, which follows the laws of thermodynamics. Which state that energy is unborn and eternal, but energy can be converted from one form to another form with a successive loss of energy at every transfer. The energy can be defined as capacity to do work, the energy at rest is known as potential energy, the energy at work is known as kinetic energy. Within the framework of these two energy, all other fundamental forms of energy, such as magnetic, electric, gravitational, heat and metabolic energy are working in the universe under the laws of thermodynamics. Laws of thermodynamics also state, when there is an increase it must be balanced by a decrease somewhere else. It means from energy point of view whole universe is a single unit we are only a small part of the same.

b. The Vedic Concept

The creation is an integral system of complex processess within it, which develops gradually and reaches at its peak, through actions and interactions in a cyclic manner. The process of the creation get start from a fundamental energy, it gets activate resulting in the formation of charged particles, the same has been depicted as evolution from non existence to existence, which is the first germ of the creation. The fundamental particles constitute the primeval nature. With the association of fundamental energy they produces atoms, molecules and the substances, the same has been depicted through the syllables in a symbolic fashion by *Ek padi, Dvi padi, Tripadi, Chatushpadi, Gāyatri, Triṣtubh, Anushtubh* and *Jagati*.

She that was fourth set Agni-and-soma; the seers arranging the(two) wings of the sacrifice- Gayatri, tristubh, jagati, anustubh, brahadark, bringing heaven(svar) for the sacrificer.Atharvaveda 8.9.14.

गायत्रस्य समिधस्तिस्न आहुस्ततो मह्ना प्र रिरिचे महित्वा। अथ. 9-10-3

Gayatri hath, they say, three bands for kindling: hence it excels in majesty and vigour. A. 9-10-3

तस्यो इन्द्रो वत्स आसीद् गायंयभिधान्यभ्रमूधः।। अथ. 8-10-5

Of her the *Indra* electricity was young *vatsa* (Son) and *Gayatri* the halter, cloud the *udder* (milk). Ath. 8.10.5

The creative power of the creation is in the three bands of *Gayatri. The Gayatri* has been identified as energy its three bands are electron, proton and neutron. *Soma* is father and *Indra* became his son, it means magnetic energy and electricity together generates electromagnetic bond energy, where magnetic energy is frist, hence the Soma has been termed as father and Indra as son,which together produces atoms and the molecules. For the creation these three fundamental particles are having milk like nourishing power through the formation of atoms, which has been indicated.

c. The Source of the Creator

सूर्य आत्मा जगत्श्चक्षुश्च।

Sun is the eye and soul of the creation.

It means what ever is going on in the creation is due to the sun. Now it is also a fact that sun is the main energy source in our solar system, further the Vedic seers says that the creative power of the sun is in *Gayatri* Atharva veda 9.10.3 and 8.10.12.

It has been said that he drives the sun and other planeta like a wheel of the chariot.

स सूर्यः पर्युरु वरांस्येन्द्रों ववृत्याद्रथ्येव चक्रा । ऋ. 10-89-2

He: throughout the wide expanses shall India turn him, swift as car-wheels, hither.

It means that they are drawing attention towards a force, which is responsible for the creativity of the sun and the force, which is responsible for the planetary movement in the solar system. Where Gayatri represents fundamenal particles.

How the fundamental energy is working in the creation, it has been indicated through a reciprocal interrelation ship of father and the son in the form of a riddles.

This beautiful one (F) (is) unaging, an immortal in the house of a mortal; for whom she (was) made, he lies; he who made(her) grew old. Ath. 10-8-26.

The life energy has been described as beautiful, un aging and immortal. It has been indicated that with the reproductive capacity of the cells, the life enrgy became young and the old cells under go aging.Ath. 10-8-26.

Both their father, or also their son; both the chief or also the meanest (Kanishth) of them; the one god, who has entered in to the mind, born the first, and he within the womb. Ath. 10-8-28.

The fundamental energy gets generated first in the atoms and in the womb. it has been termed as first born, than the fundamental energy proliferate along with the electrostatic energy of the nucleus as electromagnetic bond energy. They together have been termed as both the father and their son metaphorically. The electromagnetic energy is present in the universe and at the micro level, it is present in the atoms. Hence it has been termed as chief as well as minute (kanishth)

The full from the full he bends up (ud-ac); the full is poured with the full; also that may we know today, whence that is poured out. Ath. 10.8.29.

It has been indicated that the fundamental energy is complete in it self and it remains constant in all the state. "Whence that is poured out", it means one should know when it get generated first. Ath. 10.8.29. The answer has been given through the first born in the womb (centre).

7
The Evolution of the Creation

The creation came in to existence through evolution from an fundamental energy, which was only one in the precosmic stage, qualm and quite (Rg. 10.129). The process has been indicated symbolically. The fundamental energy has been described as the Creator, *Prajāpati, Hiraṇyagarbha* and *Pursuṣa* in *Puruṣa sukta*, in the creation hymns of *Ṛgveda*. In *Atharvaveda* same has been described as *Brahma, Skambh* and *Prajāpati* in the cosmological hymns. Vedic seers have traced the evolution of the creation from the original source that is from the fundamental energy in a systematic manner, they have postulated the fact that the creation is the manifestation of one single energy. Besides the *Vedic* seers have also mentioned about the basic principles of the creation and have described it as an system, which is self sufficient and self regulated. The great scientist Einstein through his equation $E=mc^2$ has clearly indicated that matter and energy can be converted vice versa.

If we summarize the Vedic cosmology according to the cosmogonic hymns in the light of modern knowledge than the origin of the universe was there from non- existence (*asat*), where in the beginning nothing was existed neither heaven nor earth nor atmosphere only deep darkness was there Rg. 10.129. It is the indication of the precosmic conditon prevailing prior to the origin of the creation. The one primordial substance (*ekami*) was get produced by heat, which is the first seed of desire of that one. It signifies that in the beginning from the fundamental energy, heat energy get generated, the same has been depicted as the manifestation of one from the non existence to the existence, the desire is a metaphor for the transformation of energy.. Rg. 10.129.1.

Where there was no sign of breath, the breathless breathed by its own nature (Rg. 10.129.2). It means due to the movements within it, heat gets generated at its own primarily, which is the first transformation of energy or the first manifestation of the un born energy from non existent to existent, the same is commonly known as desire of unborn and first germ of the creation Rg. 10.129.3.4.

The heat, which was being generated in the beginning get spreads in all directions Rg.10.129.5 and has produced the charged elementary particles. The formation of the charged elementary particles has been depicted as the manifestation of micro nature from the nonexistence, which became the source of nature and natural forces. *Under the nature, there are all creatures, who are moving according to their actions, above them is unborn begetter means father.* Here the unborn fundamental energy has been regarded as the father and controller of the nature as well as the creator of the creation Rg. 10.129.6.

The Vedic seers have concluded this hymn with this that who verily knows that how the creation came in to existance, he the unborn, whether he has formed it or did not form it.

The unborn energy, which is omnipotent in the univers, he verily knows it or perhaps he knows not Rg. 10.129.7.

We find more information regarding the evolution of the creation in Rg.10.72.

It has been said that *Brahmanaspati* forged together this world like a iron smith. From the nonexistence, the existence became manifested. It has been indicated metaphorically that the Brahanaspati has produced the existence from the non existence just like a iron smith produces iron by smelting. Which indicates the formation of the atoms in the primitive conditions, where with the condensation of the heat energy charged particles are get generated. The Brahanaspati here represents the nucleus, around which electrons move. Which produces atoms. Which is the state of existence of the non existence, where elctromagnetic bond energy bind the atoms. The same is the productive power, through which nature and the solar system get established, it has been indicated symbolically.

*Thence in succession arose the earth, the spaces, **Aditi** with Daksha; and after **Aditi** the Gods were born. The Gods then brought the sun. There were eight sons of **Aditi**, but eighth, **Martand**, she cast away; she brought him to be born and to die*. Here *Aditi* - nature has been described in its various stages, with the emergence of existentence micro nature came in to existence, from *Aditi*-(micro *nature) Deva*- (Gods) were born. It means fundamental particles of the nature (electron ,proton and neutron) became active with the condensation of heat energy. Which constitute micronature-(*Aditi*) in the early primitive conditions. From (*Aditi*) micronature *Dakṣa* was born. *Dakṣa* here represents Nebula, from *Dakṣa*, Solar system came in to existence, accordingly nature came into its full function, which has been indicated through reciprocal interrelationship of *Aditi* and *Dakṣa*. *Aditi* represents nature and our solar system is a part of nature, accordingly how the solar system came in to existence has been indicated through the eight sons of *Aditi*. The eight sons of *Aditi* are eight planets, out of which, she cast away *Martand,* to be born and to die. It means among the planets of solar system earth is different in the sense that life and death on the surface of the earth is its regular feature, hence *Martand* here may represent the earth. Otherwise *Martand* means sun. Gods-*Deva,* then brought forward the sun, it indicates about the nuclear reactions at the surface of the sun, which has been indicated through the dancing atoms. "When ye, O Gods, in yonder deep close clasping one another stood. Thence, as of dancers, from your feet a thickening cloud of dust arose." Here the formation of the atoms has been shown through clouds, due to the activity of *Deva*-fundamental particles, the nuclear reactions have brought the sun in action.

In a similar fashion Golden embryo-*Hiraṇya-garbha* represents the solar nebula as well as the fundamental energy, which gets generated due the movements of the particles in the Nebula, the same has been described as the lord of all that who moves or stand. It means whatever object is there, it has fundamental energy within it. Rg.10.121. *Hiraṇya-garbha*-Golden embryo signifies that in the center of the atoms and in the womb of livingbeings, the fundamental energy gets generated due to the spinning of the electrons around the nucleus in a atom and due to the streaming of protoplasm in the living cell as a life energy. As such the fundamental energy is an original source and cause of the creation, being generated in the womb(in the centre) at its own, hence it has been termed as *Hiranya-garbha* - Golden embryo.

In the *Viṣwakarma Sukta* Rg.10.81, 82, the fundamental energy has been described as the creator, accordingly the origin of the creation has been traced, the same has been described as lord of living beings *Prajapati* Rg. 10.129.

References Rigveda 1.10.72

Let us with tuneful skill proclaim these generations of the Gods (natural forces), that one may see them when theṣe hymns are chanted in a future age.1

The Brahmanaspati produced with blast and smelting like a smith. Existence in an earlier age of Gods (natural forces), from Nonexistence sprang.2

Existence, in the earlier age of Gods, from Nonexistence sprang. There after were the regions born. This sprang from the productive power.3

Earth sprang from the productive power; the regions from the earth were born.

Daksha was born of Aditi and Aditi is Child of Daksha.4

For Aditi, O Daksha, she who is thy daughter was brought forth. After her were thew blessed Gods (natural forces) born sharers of immortal life.5

When ye, O Gods, in yonder deep close clasping one another stood. Thence, as of dancers, from your feet a thickening cloud of dust arose. Here formation of the atoms has been shown.6

When, O ye like Yatis, ye caused all existing things to grow, Then ye brought Surya forward who was lying hidden in the sea.7

Eight are the sons of Aditi who from her body sprang to life. With seven she went to meet the God: she cast martand far away.8

So with her seven sons Aditi went forth to meet the earlier age. She brought martanda thitherward to spring to life and die again. Rg. 10.72.9

नासदासीन्नो सदासीत्तदानीं नासीद्रजो नो व्योमा परो यत्।

किमावरीवः कुह कस्यशर्मन्नम्भः किमासीद्गहनं गभीरम्।। ऋ. 10.129.1

Then was not non existent nor existent: there was no realm of air, no sky beyond it.

What covered in, and where? and what gave shelter ? Was water there, unfathomed depth of water?

न मृत्युरासीदमृतं न.तर्हि न रात्र्या अह्न आसीत्प्रकेतः।

आनीदवातं स्वधया तदेकं तस्माद्धान्यन्न परः किं चनास।। ऋ. 10.129.2

Death was not then, nor was there aught immortal: no sign was there, the day's and night's divider.

That One Thing: breathless, breathed by its own nature: apart from it was nothing whatsoever.

तम आसीत्तमसा गूळहमग्रेऽप्रकेतं सलिलं सर्वमा इदम्।

तुच्छये नाभ्वपिहितं यदासीत्तपसस्तन्महिनाजायतैकम्।। ऋ. 10.129.3

Darkness there was: at first concealed in darkness this All was indiscriminated chaos.

All that existed then was void and formless: by the great power of Warmth (heat) was born that Unit.

कामस्तदग्रे समवर्तताधि मनसो रेतः प्रथमं यदासीत्।

सतो बन्धुमसति निरविन्दन्हृदि प्रतीष्या कवायो मनीषा।। ऋ. 10.129.4

Thereafter rose Desire in the beginning, Desire, the primal seed and germ of Spirit.

Sages who searched with their heart's thought discovered the existent's kinship in the non-existent.

तिरश्चीनो विततो रश्मिरेषामधः स्विदासी३दुपरि स्विदासी३त्।

रेतोधा आसन्महिमान आसन्त्स्वधा अवस्तात्प्रयतिः परस्तात्।। ऋ. 10.129.5

Transversely was their severing line extended: what was above it then, and what below it?

There were begetters, there were mighty forces, free action here and energy up yonder.

को अद्धा वेद क इह प्र वोचत्कुत आजाता कुत इयं विसृष्टिः।

अर्वाग्देवा अस्य विसर्जनेनाथा को वेद यत आबभूव।। ऋ. 10.129.6

Who verily knows and who can here declare it, whence it was born and whence comes this creation?

The Gods are later than this world's production. Who knows then whence it first came into being.

इयं विसृष्टिर्यत आबभूव यदि वा दधे यदि वा न।

यो अस्याध्यक्षः परमे व्योमन्त्सो अङग् वेद यदि वा न वेद।। ऋग्वेद 10.129.7

He the first origin of this creation, whether he formed it all or did not form it.

Whose eye controls this world in highest heaven, he verily knows it, or perhaps he knows not.

8

The Creation as an Integral System

The creation is a system, which is working under the space, time and environmental conditions through cosmic ptinciples. The same has been expressed symbolically in the Vedic hymns.

Puruṣa Sukta is most important hymn of the whole Vedic literature, which symbolically reveals the secret of creation in only sixteen stanza. In *Puruṣa Sukta*-fundamental energy has been described as the personal life giving principle, as well as the orignal source of the creation, which pervades the universe. Accordingly the integrity of the individual soul and *Brahma* get established in the Upnishads.

With the knowledge of the cosmogony and cosmology of cosmos, the fundamental energy has been imagined in the form of a *Puruṣa* and the Vedic seers have described the origin of the creation from the same. Through the reciprocal intrrelationship of the Purusa and the universe. they have indicated about its inter connections with the universe.

a. Laws of Thermodynamics

The Laws of Thermodynamics have been indicated in *Puruṣa Sukta* (Rg.10.90.1 to 4), where the fundamental energy has been imagined in the form of a *Puruṣa,* with innumerable head, eyes and feet, who pervades the earth and the world and even above and in ten finger wide space. (which metaphorically indicates that this fundamental energy-*Puruṣa* is omni potent, omnipresent and eternal.)

The *purusa* is all this and that what is and what is to be, his three fourth part is in the heaven and only its one fourth part is born and reborn through transformation. Rg. 10.90.1 to 4.

Here it has been said that the *Puruṣa*-fundamental energy is universally present.

This *Puruṣa* is all that yet hath been and that is to be;

The Lord of Immortality, which waxes greater still by food. Rg. 10.90.2.

Here it has been said that the fundamental energy is eternal, the lord of immortality means it remaqins constant in the all state, but with transformation it increases, which is its food.

So mighty is his greatness; yea greater than this is *Puruṣa*. All creatures are one-fourth of him, three-fourths eternal life in heaven. Rg. 10.90.3.

Here it has been said that the cosmos is like a vast ocean of fundamental energy, the visible world is only onefourth part of him, rest three fourth part of it is in the heaven above the visible world.

With three fourths *Puruṣa* went up: one fourth of him again was here. Thence he strode out to every side over what eats not and what eats. Rg. 10.90.4.

Here it has been said that its three fourth part is invisible in the heaven, only its onefourth part is under going transformation again and again, which spreads on every side as animate and inanimate creation.

Tracing the evolution from the fundamental energy symbolically in the form of a *Puruṣa*, with this it has been also indicated that the human body is a microcosm in side a macrocosm.

सहस्रशीर्षा पुरुषः सहस्राक्षः सहस्रपात् ।

स भूमिं विश्वतो वृत्वात्यतिष्ठद्दशाङ्गुलम् ॥ ऋग्वेद 10-90-1

A Thousand heads hath *Purush,* a thousand eyes,

A thousand feet on every side pervading earth he fills a space ten fingers wide. Rig. 10.90.2.

पुरुष एवेदं सर्वं यदभूतं यच्च भाव्यम् ।

उतामृतत्वस्येशानो यदन्नेतिरोहति॥ ऋग्वेद 10.90.2

This *Puruṣa* is all that yet hath been and all that to be;
The lord of Immortality which waxes greater still by food.

एतावानस्य महिमातो ज्यायाँश्च पुरूषः।

पादोस्य विश्वा भूतानि त्रिपादस्यामृतं दिवि ॥ ऋग्वेद 10.90.3

So mighty is his greatness; yea, greater than this is *Puruṣa*.
All creatures are one-fourth of him, three-fourths eternal life in heaven.

त्रिपादूर्ध्व उदैत्पुरूणः पादोऽस्येहाभवत्पुनः ।

ततो विण्वङ्व्यक्रामत्साशनानशने अभि ॥ ऋग्वेद 10.90.4

With three-fourths *Puruṣa* went up : one forth of him again was here.

Thence he strode out to every side over what eats not and what eats.

ण्यज्ञेन यज्ञमयजन्त देवास्तानि धर्माणि प्रथमान्यासन् ।

ते ह नाकं महिमानः सचन्त यत्र पूर्वे साध्याः सन्ति देवाः॥ ऋग्वेद 10.90.16

The God sacrificing, sacrificed the victim: these were the earliest holy Ordinances.

In the same continuity under the influence of nature through complexity of actions and inter-actions, life has its origin at its own on the earth. With the evolution of the living beings, the system became self sufficient and self regulated. It means the creation is the transformation of an energy, which has been indicated.

इन्द्रं मित्रं वरूणमग्निमाहुरथो दिव्यः स सुपर्णो गरूत्मान्।

एकं सद्विप्रा बहुधा वदन्त्यग्निं यमं मातरिश्वानमाहुः ॥ ऋग्वेद 1.164.46

They call him *Indra, Mitra, Varuna, Agni* and he is heavenly nobly winged *Garutman.*

To what is one, sages give many a title: they call it *Agni, Yama, Matarisvan.*

The one energy is called by the seers with different names, means all are the different forms of a single energy.

b. Cosmic Principles

Cosmic principles–In the last two stanza cosmic principle of action and interaction have been given, under which creation is working as a system.

Gods sacrificing sacrificed the victim—these were the earliest ordinances. The mighty ones attained height of heaven, there where the *Sadhyas*, Gods of old, are dwelling. Rg. 10.90.16.

The *Yajna*-sacrifice means action and interactions, here it has been said that from actions and interactions again actions and interactions get generated, where according to the cosmic law, *Deva*-fundamental particles are the first, with their activity they get reached to the height of matter and the fundamental particles-*Deva*. It means initially the fundamental particles are the first in the series of action and interactions, through their activity they gets converted into the matter and again reached to their original old state of *Deva*-fundamental particle, which indicates about the natural cycles, through which the natural components get synthesized and disintegrated in the reversible direction.

Seven fencing-sticks had he, thrice seven layers have been prepared, When the Gods, offering sacrifice, bound, as their victim, *Puruṣa.* Rg. 10.90.15.

Here it has been expressed that the process of creation has get initiated, when fundamental particles get bind in a atom, where due to the spinning of the electrons around the nucleus ectromagnetic energy get generated in the atoms, in this way the fundamental energy (*Puruṣa)* get bound in side the atoms, which binds the atoms. Accordingly the creation came in to existence. For the functions of the creation seven sticks (seven planets), twenty one fuel get prepared, these twenty one fuel represents twelve months, six seasons, three weather. Through which creation is working as a system, it has three centers-sky, atmosphere, earth as indicated by the three layers. In this way a picture of the creation system has been expressed symbolically.

c. Oxidation and Reduction

In the nature a number of chemical chain reactions are going on, all the substances which are present in the nature are the by products of the same. These substances, whether simple or complex, when degraded became converted in to the fundamental particles of the earliest order, from where the substances were get synthesized.

In the Atharvaveda questions have been raised regarding the secret of creation, accordingly the answers have been given by the seers. Which indicates about the nature of chemical and biochemical reactions in a symbolic fashion.

यो वेतसं हिरण्ययं तिष्ठन्तं वेद ।

स वै गुह्यः प्रजापतिः ॥ अथर्ववेद 10.7.41

He who knows the golden reed *Vatsa* standing in the sea-he varily is in secret *Prajapati*, means the person who knows the root cause of the creation, that how it get sustained, he varily, knows secret *Prajapati*, means he has the knowledge of the fundamental energy.

तन्त्रमेकें युवती विरूपे अभ्याक्रामं वयतः षणमयूखम।

प्रान्या तन्तूंस्तिरते धत्ते अन्या नाप वृञ्जाते न गमातो अन्तम्॥ अथर्ववेद 10.7.42

A certain pair of maidens, of diverse form, weave, betaking themselves to it, the six-pegged web; the one draws forth the threads *tantu*, the other sets [them]; they wrest not off (*apa-vrj*), they go not to an end.

How the creation has been sustained, the answer has been given in a symbolic fashion in the form of a maiden pair of diverse nature. It means the two fundamental reactions of the nature, which are going on alternately. These two are the oxidation and reduction reactions . In the living organisms they are known as the anabolism and catabolism. The anabolism is related with the reduction and synthesis of the complex substances, the catabolism is related with the oxidation and simplification of the complex substances. These two diverse types of reactions are operating universally in the universe simultaneously one after the another. The synthesis and destruction is the law of nature, which through actions and interactions in all six directions, weave a web, commonly known as food web in the nature. One weave it and other destroy it , it means anabolism and another draws forth the threads means catabolism. In this way these two reactions never reached to an end whether in the nature or in the living beings. The difference is only this that inside the living beings they are operating in the presence of enzymes, which lower down the energy of activation of the molecules. Outside the cells, the molecules requires more energy for the activation. In this way this stanza reveals the fact that how the creation get sustained.

तयोरहं परिनृत्यन्त्योरिव न वि जानामि यतरा परस्तात्।

पुमानेनद् वयत्युङ्गृणति पुमानेनद वि जमाराधि नाके।। अथर्ववेद 10.7.43

Of them, as of two women dancing about, I do not distinguish (*vi-jna*) which is beyond; a man (*pumans*), weaves it, ties [it] up; a man hath borne it about upon the firmament (*naka*).

Here these reactions have been described as two dancing women. out of two, which one is beyond is difficult to say but a *Puruṣa*-fundamental energy weave it ties (it) up the same has spread it in the sky.

Here the Vedic seers have clearified further that no one can say that which reaction is first, because these two reactions operate simultaneously in nature. Further they have given indications through *Puruṣa*-fundamental energy that the stability of the substances or matter is due to the the *Puruṣa* fundamental energy, it signifies the bond energy, which is responsible for the synthesis and degradation of the matter, who has spread up it in the sky and in all the directions.

इमे मयूखा उप तस्तभुर्दिवं सामानि चक्रुस्तसराणि वातवेः। अथर्ववेद 10.7.44

These pegs propped up the sky; the chants they made shuttles for weaving.

It has been indicated here that these oxidation reduction cycles have brought the creation in the existence. Where the substrates are the means for the same, here the chants signifies the substrates. Ath. 10.7.44.

d. The Solar System in the Riddles

Most of the knowledge, which have deep concern with creation have been expressed through riddles and their answers are also in the form of riddles. Rg. 1.164 is having only 52 stanzas. Which have almost full knowledge of the creation. Vedic seers, under the laws of phonetics have developed the language code in the form of metaphors and riddles, so that maximum information may be coded in the hymns. It is also evident from the fact that during the compilation of the hymns to save a single syllable was equivalent to the celebration as that birth of a male child. Accordingly it was possible to express full knowledge of the creation in only sixteen stanza as in *Puruṣa Sukta* Rg. 10.90 or Rg. 1.164, having fifty two stanza.

Of this pleasant (*vama*) hoary invoker-of him the brother is the midmost (*acna*); his third brother is Ghee backed (*Ghrit prishtha*); there I saw the seven sons of chief of the world Rg. 1.164.1.

The first riddle gives the idea about the creation that the supreme fundamental energy, who has been invoked in the creation sacrifice, guarded by him (sun), his middle brother *is Ashnaha*–air, his third brother *is Ghrit pristha*–organic matter. Here I have seen seven sons of the *Vishwapatim*–The chief of the world. Rg.1-164-1, the seven sons are seven rays, who feed the life on the earth. In this way the Vedic seers have drawn the attention towards three main centers of the creation sky (sun), air- atmosphere and plants on the earth, the plants which synthesise organic matter have been termed as ghrit prashtha.

Seven harness (*yuj*) a one wheeled chariot; one horse, having seven names, draw (*vah*) it; of three naves (is) the wheel unwasting, unassiled where on stand all these existence. Rg. 1.164.2.

The seven harness, who yoke the chariot are seven planets of the solar system, which is one wheeled chariot. One horse having seven names is sun, who has seven visible rays and is responsible for the working of the solar system. The three naves are sun in the sky, who feed the creation through its nuclear reactions at its surface, the second nave of the creation is the middle atmosphere, where magnetospheric processes feed the creation through ionization, its third nave is on the earth, where plants nourish the living beings at its surface through their autotrophic nature. On these three naves (centers) the creation has its existence.

The seven they stand on this chariot- seven horses draw it, seven wheeled; seven sisters shout it together, where are set down the seven names of the kine.

The solar system has been termed as a chariot, where seven planets of the solar system drive the solar system through their movement around the sun as horse, the planets are rotating at their axis, due to this they have magnetic field and the magnetosphere around them, which is responsible for the movement of the solar system, hence they have been termed as wheels of the chariot. The seven sisters are seven visible rays, who feed the living beings like a cow on the earth. Rg. 1.164.3.

Another very interesting riddle is-let him who truly knows (here) tell the set down track of this pleasant bird; the kine extract milk from his head; clothing themselves in a wrap, they drunk water with the foot.

The places of the pleasant bird-(sun), from where the kine extract the milk from his head. The visible solar rays (VIBGYOR), which are coming on the earth's surface from the head of the sun are being trapped by the plants for the photosynthesis, which acts as milk through nourishment for the living beings, hence the visible rays of the sun have been compared with the kine, the absorption of water by the green plants has been indicated through the drinking of water with the foot, who represents root system. Rg. 1.164.7.

9
The Regulator of The Creation

a. The Sacrifice-*Yajna*

The creation has came in to existence through the evolution from an fundamental energy, which regulates it through the *Yajna* and the creation has been described as *Srishti Yajna.* Where the power of the creation is in the fundamental particles.

The creative power of the sun is in *Gayatri* Atharvaveda 9.10.3 and 8.10.12. It has been said that he drives the sun and others like a wheel of the chariot. It indicates about the existence of a fundamental energy.

स सूर्यः पर्युरु वरांस्येन्द्रों ववृत्यादथ्येव चक्रा । ऋ. 10.89.2

He : throughout the wide expanses shall Indra turn him, swift as car-wheels, hither.

गायत्रस्य समिधस्तिस्र आहुस्ततो मह्ना प्र रिरिचे महित्वा। अथ. 9.10.3

Gayatri hath, they say, three bands for kindling: hence it excels in majesty and vigour. Ath. 9.10.3

तस्यो इन्द्रो वत्स आसीद् गायत्र्यभिधान्यभ्रमूधः।। अथ 8.10.5

Of her the *Indra* electricity was young *vatsa* (Son) and *Gayatri* the halter, cloud the *udder* (milk). Ath. 8.10.5

The creative power of the creation is in the three bands of *Gayatri*. *Gayatri* has been identified as energy its three bands are electron, proton and neutron. *Soma* is father and *Indra* became his son, it means magnetic energy and electricity together generates electromagnetic bond energy, where magnetic energy is frist, which produces atoms and the molecules. For the creation these three fundamental particles are having milk like nourishing power through the formation of the atoms, which has been indicated here.

Different types of atoms and substances are get formed under the temperature pressure gradient through actions and interactions, the same has been depicted by the imagination in the form of syllables. Ath. 8.9.14.

अग्नीषोमावदधुर्या तुरीयासीद् यज्ञस्य पक्षावृषयः कल्पयन्तः।

गायत्रीं त्रिष्टुभं जगतीमनुष्टुभं बृहदर्की यजमानाय स्वराभरन्तीम्।। अथ 8.9.14

She that was fourth set *Agni-Soma.* The seers arranging the wings of the sacrifice as *Gayatri, Trishtubh, Jagati anushtubh, brahadarki,* bringing heaven for the sacrificer.

Here it has been indicated that for the purpose of creation sacrifice by *Agni-Soma* which filled the space have been imagined in the form of syllables *Gayatri, Trishtubh Jagati, anushtubh and brahadarki* which indicates the constitution of the atoms, molecules and the substances symbolically.

Yajna signifies actions and interactions at micro level in the nature. In the creation verious types of reactions are going on in cyclic manner, which are responsible for origin of the creation under the influence of heat and cold. Accordingly the Vedic seers have described creation as creation sacrifice *Sristi Yajna.* The same has been indicated in the very first verse of Rigveda.

अग्निमीळे पुरोहितं यज्ञस्य देवमृत्विजम्। होतारं रत्नघातमम्।। १।।

I call *Agni*-Energy, which is priest, deity and (Rtvij) the invoker of the sacrifice, the best bestower of treasure.

Here sacrifice signifies the creation sacrifice. It means actions and inter-actions, which are going on in the creation, through which creation came in to existence. Here the energy, which is being invoked is fundamental energy, from where the process of creation get started, through the energy transformation, the fundamental energy has been described as unborn, omnipotent and omnipresent, the same is the priest, Deva-God and reciter (invoker) of the creation sacrifice. It means the energy, which initiates the creation sacrifice and the fundamental particles. They are the source of various substances of the creation.

Ruler of the *Sristi Yajna*-fundamental energy increases at its own and its activities are under *Ṛta*-Cosmic principle. Rg.1.1.8.

The process of creation is under the cosmic principles, where the energy increases at its own it means it increases with transformation, for which there is no external force. Here the Vedic seers have indicated about the functions of the creation.

In the vedic terminology the sacrifice-*Yajna* signifies actions and interactions at micro level at a length in the universe, the vedic sacrificial ritual commonly known as *Karm kandiya Yajna* for daily sacrifice is a model of it.

यो यज्ञो विश्वतस्तन्तुभिस्तत एकशतं देवकर्मेभिरायतः।

इमे वयन्ति पितरो य आययुः प्र वयाप वयेत्यासते तते।। ऋ. 10.130.1

The sacrifice drawn out with threads on every side, stretched by a hundreds sacred ministers and one.

This do these father weave who hither-ward are come: they sit beside the warp and cry, Weave forth, weave back.

The whole creation is depicted as the *Yajna*-sacrifice, in which the earth is *Vedi*-altar for the creation sacrifice. The creation sacrifice gets elaborated with the threads on every side, stretched by a hundred and one sacred ministers. It has been indicated here that hundred and one elements are working in the nature. Through their activity the living creatures have came in to existence. Which have generated food webs and food chains in the nature.

पुमाँ एनं तनुत उत्कृणत्ति पुमान्वि तत्ने अधि नाके अस्मिन्।

इमे मयूखा उप सेदुरू सदः सामानि चक्रुस्तसराण्योतवे।। ऋ. 10.130.2

Man extend and the man unbind it even in heaven and sky, in which the *Soma* is the weaving shuttle for these pegs.

The *Soma* signifies bond energy, which is responsible for the stability of the atoms, molecules and the substances. *Puman* signifies *Puruṣa*-fundamental energy. It means the synthesis and degradation of the complex substances has been attributed to the fundamental bond energy.

In the creation sacrifice the earth has been termed as sacrificial hearth, which is the main place for the actions and interactions. Where heat and cold are the two fire and the rain water acts as butter, accordingly the sun is the source of the sacrifice, which has been indicated in the Atharvaveda. Ath. 13.1.47.

हिमं घ्रंसं चाधाय यूपान् कृत्वा पर्वतान्।

वर्णाज्यावग्नी ईजाते रोहितस्य स्वर्विदः॥ अर्थववेद 13.1.47

Having set cold and heat, having made the mountains sacrificial posts (*Yupa*), having rain as sacrifical butter, the two fires of the sky finding ruddy one (sun) performed sacrifice (*Yagnya*).

वेदि भूमि कल्पयित्वा दिवं कृत्वा दक्षिणाम्।

घ्रंसं तदग्निं कृत्वा चकार विश्वमात्मन्वद् वर्षेणाज्येन रोहितः॥ अर्थववेद 13.1.52

Having shaped the earth as sacrificial hearth, having made the sky sacrificial fee, then having made heat his fire, the ruddy one made all that has soul, with rain as sacrificial butter.

The earth has been described as the place for sacrifice, where the heat energy is acting as fire and the rain is like butter. It means water and temperature are the two main factors, through which the living creatures have came in to existence.

यज्ञेन यज्ञमयजन्त देवास्तानि धर्माणि प्रथमान्यासन् ।

ते ह नाकं महिमानः सचन्त यत्र पूर्वे साध्याः सन्ति देवाः॥ ऋग्वेद 10.90.16

This stanza indicates that in the creation, the cyclic chain reactions are going on, in which the reaction products are act as substrate for the next reaction. It means in the nature ions, atoms and molecules, which initiates the formation of different complex susbtances, ultimately they will be converted in to the same state in a cyclic manner.

All the complex substances in the nature and the living beings are the products of two main types of reactions known as oxidation and reduction, through which the creation is working as an system, the same has been indicated beautifully in a symbolic fashion, through a metaphor of dancing girls.

तन्त्रमेकें युवती विरूपे अभ्याक्रामं वयतः षण्मयूखम।

प्रान्या तन्तूंस्तिरते धत्ते अन्या नाप वृञ्जाते न गमातो अन्तम्॥ अथर्ववेद 10.7.42.

It has been indicated here that two reactions of diverse nature. They are the regulator of the nature, which has given it a shape of web, in which one reaction is related with the synthesis and other with simplication means oxidation and reduction known as anabolism and catabolism in the living beings, which has been indicated as one weave and other set like a cloth web in the sky but do not reach to their destiny. It means the oxidation and reduction reactions operates in a cyclic manner, which are going on continuously in the nature. These reactions like dancing girls rotate in different directions. Ath. 10.7.43. It means they produces many cyclic reactions, in which, which is the first reaction either the oxidation or reduction, it cann't be said. A *Purusa*-fundamental energy weaves it and ties it up. It means the bond energy is responsible for the binding and the same is responsible for its degradation. Where heat and cold initiates the reactions.

How the creation is sustained, how it gets regulated? who supports it? The answers have been given in a single stanza.

इमामेणां पृथिवीं वस्त एकोऽन्तरिक्षं पर्येको बभूव।

दिवमेणां ददते यो विधर्ता विश्वा आशाः प्रति रक्षन्त्येकें।। अर्थववेद 10.8.36

One of them clothes himself in this earth; one encompassed the atmosphere; of he them who is disposer *Vidhatra* gives the sky, some defend respectively all regions.

One, which is in the earth and cover the earth is the geomagnetic field of the earth, who protects the earth from the solar wind and one encompass the atmosphere is ozone layer, which absorbs UV radiations and protects the earth from the toxic rays. He of them one is regulator, who gives the sky, it means oxidation and reduction reactions, who regulates the creation, due to its by products the sky has its existence. One defend all regions accordingly, it means the magnetosphere of earth's magnetic field, which defend the earth from magnetic fields of the sun and other planets from all the sides.

Due to the presence of chlorophyll in plants, they are known as autotrophs and radiant energy of sun get converted in to the chemical energy. The presence of chlorophyll in the plants has been indicated through Avi. Ath.10.8.31

अविर्वै नाम देवतर्तेनास्ते परीवृता।

तस्या रूपेणेमे वृक्षा हरिता हरितस्रजः।। अथर्ववेद 10.8.31

The deity *Avi* by name sits enveloper with right; by her form these trees [are] green, green-garlanded. Ath. 10.8.31

महद् यक्षं भुवनस्य मध्ये तपसि क्रान्तं सलिलस्य पृष्ठे।

तस्मिन् छ्रयन्ते यउकेच देवा वृक्षस्य स्कन्धः परित इवशाखाः।। अथर्ववेद 10.7.38

The great monster *Yaksa* is in the midst of the creation *Bhuvana* Stroda *Krant* in penace on the back of the sea in it are set (cvi) whatever Gods these are like the branches of a tree round about the trunk.

It has been indicated here that in the mid of the creation, the fundamental energy is like a Yaksa, who supports all the natural forces of nature, through its interconnections.

In the Asya Wamiya Sukta-The hymn of the supreme Rgveda 1.164, a detailed analysis of the creation has been described in the form of riddles and metaphors, where questions been asked and their answers have been given through metaphors, one such metaphor is Yajna-sacrifice, which is a model, through which answers have been given. Rg. 1.164.34.

That I ask thee of the earth's extremist end, where is the centre of the creation, I ask thee. I ask thee Stallions's seed prolofic, I ask of highest heaven where speech abideth.

Yajna vedi is earth's extremist end, it means through the series of actions and interactions the earth has came in to existence and it will go to its end through the same series of actions and interactions as going on in the Yagnya vedi. Rg. 1.164.35

The Yajna-sacrifice is the centre of the creation, it means the creation is regulated and sustained through the series of the actions and interactions in the cyclic manners as going on in the Yajna-sacrifice, hence it is the centre of the creation.

The Stallion's seed prolific is the soma, It means the force, who drive the creation, which is responsible for working of the creation is soma (magnetic energy). It means they are drawing attention towards the inter planetary magnetic field and the magnetic fields of the astronomical bodies.

The Vac-speech's highest place is in the universe, it means they are drawing attention towards imperishable nature of the Vac-speech.

पृच्छामि त्वा परमन्तं पृथिव्याः पृच्छामि यत्र भुवनस्य नाभिः ।

पृच्छामि त्वा वृष्णो अश्वस्य रेतः पृच्छामि वाचः परमं व्योम ।। ऋ. 1-164-34

इयं वेदिः परो अन्तः पृथिव्या अयं यज्ञो भुवनस्य नाभिः।

अयं सोमो वृष्णो अश्वस्य रेतो ब्रह्मायं वाचः परमं व्योम ।। ऋ. 1.164.35

b. The Time-*Kala*

In our solar system, planets are moving around the sun and they are rotating at their axis simultaneously. Rotation of the sun and earth at there axis has given the concept of *Kala*-time, the creation has came in to the existence with time, the same has been indicated in *the Kala Sukta.* Atharvaveda 19.53 & 54.

The evolution and development of the matter, which leads to the origin of life is mainly dependent on the time factor. For which universal clock is set in the sun, which is related with the rotation of the sun at its axis. When earth complets its one rotation around the sun, during that period sun rotates at its axis twelve times. These are its twelve faces, which constitute twelve months. The planetary movement and rotation of the sun, moon and earth at their axis with a fixed duration have given the concept of time as day-night, months, year and seasons, which is mainly responsible for the changes in temperature-pressure and electron density in the atmosphere. Which has triggered off number of chemical reactions in the region of ionosphere under the influence of cosmic rays, electric discharge and the geomagnetic field of the earth. Consequently the different atmospheric layers have came into the existence, which has generated the cordial conditions for the origin of life on the earth with the arrival of the seasons.

Twelve are the fellies, and the wheel single; three are the naves. What man hath understood it?

Therein are set together spokes three hundred and sixty, which in nowise can be loosened. Rg. 1.164.48

For the creation the most important event is the time, which is related with the rotation of sun at its axis. Which signifies the beginning of the creation, the same has been indicated through the wheel-*Rath*, which is moving continuously, this wheel has twelve spokes-the twelve months and three sixty nails represents the three sixty days. One complete rotation of the Sun at its axis is *known as Samvatsara Kala*-a year with twelve months. The calculation of time start with the entry of the sun in Aries rashi. Which is suppose to be the beginning point of the creation. The year have three hundred and sixty days with three centers-sun, moon and the earth.

The importance of the *Samvatsara Kala*- has been indicated through a riddle-formed with twelve spokes by length of time, unweakened, rolls round the heaven this wheel of during Order.

Herein established, joined in pairs together, seven hundred Sons and twenty stand, O Agni.

It has been indicated here that the unaging *Kala*-time is the cosmic law, under which the creation is working as an system, which has twelve month, seven hundred twenty days and night together, which constitute a year.

Today we know that a year has three sixty five days, the same has been indicated through a intercalary month and a extra season in the succession.

The whole creation is being dependent on time-*Kal.* The year (*Samvatsara*) is the chariot of it, the complete year (*Parivatsara*) is its lap (base), the *Viraj-Agni* (*Soma*) is the mouth of this chariot, *Indra* (electricity) is the left stander of the chariot, and moon is the charioteer of the chariot.(who regulate the seasons during the year). Atharvaveda 8.8.23.

It has been indicated here that every thing, which is going on in the creation is due to the Time-*Kala*, which is the main cause of the creation and is related with the rotation of the sun at its axis-Kala. The every thing and whatever is going on in the creation is attributed to the time-*Kala*. Atharvaveda 19- *Sukta* 53 and 54.

10
Genetics in the metaphors

All the living ereatures exhibits same functions at the cellular level, under which energy transformation, growth and reproduction are their natural qualities. In all the living beings RNA-Ribose Nucleic Acid or DNA-Deoxy Ribose Nucleic Acid is the main genetic material, which decides the course of life.

The credit for discovering the Deoxy Ribose Nucleic Acid goes to the Watson and Crick, which has brought a revolution in the field of biotechnology.

In the biology it is a kwon faet that in the human beings there are 23 pairs of chromosomes, in which one pair xx, or xy decides the gender and one pair is having the information for the life and death. Which regulates the life through its Genetic hereditary characters. The chromosomes consists of DNA a characteristic feature of the DNA is the fixed content and sequence of nuclotide pairs along the entire length of its double helix. In this respect any one species of DNA differ from the other species. Accordingly the species diversity is there in the nature with different hereditary characters. A definite number of nucleotides constitute a gene, which have the information about the synthesis of specific kind of the proteins. They through the enzymes regulates the metabolic reactions.

The DNA is having only four types of bases Adennine, Guanine, Thymine and Cytosine, they are arranged on the DNA spiral strips in defferent sequences. The two base Adenine and Guanine are known as purine and two base

Thymine and Cytosine are known as pyrimidine, purine and pyrimidine are complimentary with each other, such as Adenine=Thymine and Guanine≡Cytosine and vice versa. These complimentry bases are bind with each other by hydrogen double bond and triple bond. The sequence of three bases, called a triplet known as codon, with four kinds of bases in the DNA. There are 64 codes, which is known as genetic code, which is a code for aminoacid and constitute a language code for the protein synthesis. These 64 codes may constitute a language code for recording the thoughts and deeds of an individual, which is imperishable and get stimulated by the enzymes as indicated in the Veda.The DNA through transcription synthsise mRNA and mRNA through translation synthesise proteins.

The same has been expressed symbolically in the Veda, through association and interrelationships of the different forms with one another. Their relationship has been expressed through the family relationship as parents, spouse-wife, husband, offsprings, son and daughter, union of two have been indicated through Aswin.

The living cell has been termed as *Ṛbhu*, nucleus as *Brahaspati*, chromosomes as *Yama*, genetic material as *Tvastr* and *Vivasvata*.

The DNA has been termed as *Tvastr*, who is shaper of all creatures, hence it has been termed as omniform (*Visvarupa*), it means the DNA is present in all the living beings Rg.1.188.9.

Tvastr the lord hath made all forms and all the cattle of the field:Cause them to multiply for us, Rg. 1.188.9

Tvastr begot *Brahaspati* (nucleus) and has been expressed as regulator and guide. Rg. 2.23.7.

The Tvastr-DNA synthesise new DNA from the DNA template, the same has been termed as the bridal car, the single strand of the DNA template has been termed as the daughter of Tvastr and the new DNA hs been termed as *Vivasvata*. He is the father of *Aswin* (nucleotide pair), it means nucleotide pairs which get synthesized from the DNA template. He is the father of *Yama- Yami* (Twinned pair of chromosome) It means chromosomes get synthsised from the DNA. He is the father of *Manu*-human race, which signifies that DNA is responsible for the evolution of the human species. His wife is *Saranyu* daughter of *Tvastr,* who get disappear. It means the daughter represents the DNA template and after the synthesis of the mRNA, the DNA template get lost its identity, which has been expressed metaphorically.

Tvastr makes a wedding-car for his daughter; by reason of this, all this creation comes together; the mother of *Yama*, wife of great *Vivasvata*, being drawn about, disappeared. Ath. 18.1.53 The synthesis of the complimentary base pairs of the new DNA has been expressed by saying that having made one of like color, they gave her to Visvasvata.

They hid away the immortal (biosoul) one from mortals; having made one of like color, they gave her to *Vivasvata*; what that was carried also the two *Aswins (Nucleotide)* and *Saranyu* deserted two twins (Pair of chromosomes). Atharvaveda. 18.2.33.

The structure of the DNA has been indicated symbolically through Yama (chromosome),Yama's two brindled dogs four eyed watch the path of man, it means they represents two helix of the DNA and the four eyes represents two base pairs, who watch the path of man. It means the life of a individual get regulated by the information, which is there in the coded language of the DNA, simultaneously the deeds of a individual get recorded in the coded language of the DNA.

The same has been expressed in Ṛgveda also.

With Trikadrukas it purifies it self six wide ones verily great one; tristubh, gāyatri, the meters: all those (are) set in Yama. Ath. 18-2-6.

The activity of the DNA has been indicated through *Trikadruka (=, ≡),* who represents a triple bond and a double bond of hydrogen, through which the complimentary base pairs get joined with each other. 'The six wide ones' represents the three nucleotide pairs. 'The verily great one' it indicates a triplet language code on the DNA template. The language of the DNA has been indicated through the tristubh, gāyatri and the meters: all those (are) set in Yama, it means the information is in the chromosome. The triple and double hydrogen bonds play a major role in the synrhesis of mRNA and DNA duplication, which has been expressed through *Trikadruka (=, ≡).*

Originally the DNA has only four types of base, out of which three base constitute a genetic code means a code for a aminoacid for the synthesis of protein, there are 64 codes. In the Veda the triplet genetic code has been termed as three headed demon or *Trishira* the son of Visvarupa (omniform) *Tvastṛ*. Till the triplet code is in association with the DNA, it is unproductive. In the nature one of the strand of DNA acts as template for the synthesis of m RNA in the presence of the enzyme RNA polymerase, which have the coded genetic information for the protein synthesis. The base sequence in mRNA is complimentary to the base sequence in parent DNA. The synthesis of mRNA for the protein synthesis is its productive power, which initiates protein synthesis, the same has been expressed through *Trita*-triple bond, who is the slaughter of the three headed six eyed demon (three complimentary base pairs). Rg. 10.99.6.

Well skilled to use the weapons of his father *Aptya* urged on by Indra fought the battle then Trita slew the foe seven rayed three headed and freed the cattles of the son of *Tvastr*. Rg. 10.10.8.

Lord of the brave *Indra* cleft him in pieces, who sought to gain much strength and deemed him mighty. He smote his three heads from his body seizing the cattle of of the omniform *Tvastr*. Rg. 10.10.9.

The release of the cattles signifies the productivity of the mRNA, who take part in protein synthesis through genetic code, the weapons of the *Trita* is bond energy, which is being represented by *Indra* and *Aptya*-water, the triplet code is being generated due to the separation of triplet base through breaking the two double and a single triplet bond with the help of water, the same has been expressed as seven rays, which get break through *Indra* and *Aptya*, as such the codes of mRNA get translated for protein synthesis and accordingly *Tvastr's visvarupa* (omniform) get expressed.

The structure of the duplicating DNA has been expressed symbolically through *Sinivali*, who is broad hipped, fair armed, fair fingered. The broad hips represents a loop of the DNA and the two separating strips have been termed as fair arms and the projecting nucleotides are termed as her fingers. She has been invoked with *Raka, Kuhu-Gungu and Sarasvati*, where Raka represents full moon. It means a loop of the DNA is like a full moon. *Kuhu* and *Gungu* represents first day of moon, it means the separating DNA exhibits crescent shaped structures, they looks like first day of the moon. During the separation of the DNA helix in the womb a initiator code get opened which is synonym to a particular thought energy of an individual ancestor, which may get bind with the initiator code and accordingly a dead person's thought mentality may get rebirth. So it has been prayed that to a girl, O *Sinivali*, O *Sarasvati* grant her good progeny.

Stand firm; *viraj* art thou; as it were, *Vishnu* here *O Sarasvati; O Sinivali*, let her have progeny; may she be in the favor of *Bhaga*, Ath. 14.2.15.

In the Rigveda, it has been indicated that *Tvastr* give shapes to the infant in the womb and the germ is get set by the *Sinivali* and *Sarasvati* in the womb, accordingly Aswins (nucleotide pairs) crowned with lotuses, it means the development of the children will be there according to the hereditary characters, where the Sinivali is the code initiatiator and the Sarasvati (thought energy) opens the door of a language, which is particular to an individual through Aswin (nucleotide pair). It means the first code, which is present on the single strand of the DNA template, it acts as the language code initiator for a particular mentality, which is particular to a individual, hence even time twins have different characters and mentality.

1. May Visnu form and mould the womb, may Tvastr duly shape the forms. Prajapati infuse the stream and dhatar lay the germ for thee.
2. O Sinivali set the germ, set thou the germ Sarasvati. May the twain gods bestow the germ. The Aswins crowned with lotuses.
3. That which Aswin the Twain rub forth with the attrition stock of gold that germ of thine we invoke that in the tenth month thou may bear. Rg. 10.184.1, 2, 3.

Evolution through cross breeding in the living organisms is a fact, which has been indicated through a conversation between *Yama* and *Yami* symbolically, who are twin brother and sister they represents different pairs of chromosomes and crossing over between the two different strains, where *Yami* asks her brother to marry with her so as to produce offsprings and *Yama* has replied that "to marry with a sister is against the law you go to another person and encircle around him like a climber and produce offsprings."(encircle around him like a climber is a metaphor and a indication for the crossing over during meiotic cell division) (Rg. 10.10 and Atharvaveda 18.2). The same is the basis of Darwin's theory of organic evolution and Mendel's Laws of Inheritance.

The *Yama* is a king of life and death, which represents a pair of chromosome as we know that in the human beings there are twenty three pairs of chromosomes and out of it one pair, who bears the genetic information about the life and death in its genetic sequence of DNA has been termed as *Yama* and the different chromosomes have been termed as *Yama* and *Yami*, which indicates about crossing over between two different strains of chromosomes. Yama's two brindled dogs with four eyes, who watch the course of life of a man, in the modern terminology they represents two strips of the DNA and four eyes symbolically indicates about two complimentary DNA base pairs (Adenine, Guanine, Thymine and Cytosine.) A=T, G ≡ C, who records the deeds and thoughts in its genetic code sequence, which remains active through out the life and the language is imperishable. The chromosomes with their DNA base sequence maintains their continuity in the living beings through their offsprings. The coded language of the DNA may get stimulated during the DNA duplication in the womb, through the thought energy of an individual of a dead person. The same has been indicated through yama's two four eyed dogs, who watch the path of the man.

Verily the generator made us(du) in the womb man and spouse-God Tvastar, Savitar of all forms Atharvaveda; none overthrow his ordinances earth knows us (two) as such, also heaven. 18.1.5.

Yami

Desire of *Yama* hath come un to me *Yami*, in order to lying together in the same lair (yoni); I would fain yield (*ric*) my body as wife to husband*; may we whirl off, like two chariot wheels.* Atharvaveda 18-1-8.

Yama

Verily I may not mingle my body with thy body; they call him wicked (papa) who approach his sister. That is not consonant with my mind and heart, that I, a brother, should lie in a sister's bed. Atharvaveda 18-1-14

Yami

A weaking alas, art thou, O *Yama*; we have not found mind and heart thine, another woman shall embrace thee, as a girth a harnessed (Horse), as a *twinning plant (libuja) a tree.* Atharvaveda 18.1.15.

Yama

Another man, truly, O *Yami*, another man shall embrace thee as a *twinning plant a tree,* either thou seek his mind or he thine; then make for thy self very excellent concord (*samvid*). Atharvaveda 18.1.16.

Run thou past the *two four eyed, brindled dogs* of *Sarama*, by a happy road; then go unto the beneficent Fathers, who revel in common revelry with *Yama*. Atharvaveda 18-2-11.

What two defending dogs thou hast, O Yama, four eyed, sitting by the road, men watching, with them, O king, do thou surround him; assign to him well being and freedom from disease. Atharvaveda 18.2.12.

Broad nosed, feeding on lives, copper coloured, *Yama's* two messengers go about after men ((*jana*); let them give us back here today excellent life (*asu*) to see the sun. Atharvaveda 18.2.13.

They hid away the immortal (bio soul) one from mortals; having made one of like color, they gave her to *Vivasvant*; what that was carried also the two *Aswins*; and *Saranyu* deserted two twins (Pair of chromosomes). Atharvaveda 18-2-33. Tvashtar makes a wedding-car for his daughter; by reason of this, all this creation comes together; the mother of Yama, wife of great Vivasvant, being drawn about, disappeared. 18.1.53.

Tvashtar disposed (vi-dha) the garment for beauty, by direction of Brihaspati, of the poets; therewith let Savitar and Bhaga envelop this woman, like Surya, with progeny. Atharvaveda 14.1.53

With the trikadrukas it purifies itself; six wide ones, verily one great one; tristubh, gayatri, the meters; all those [are] set in Yama. Atharvaveda 18.3.6.

Yama beyond, below Vivasvant—beyond that do I see nothing whatever; into Yama has entered my sacrifice; Vivasvant stretched after the worlds (bhu). 15. stand firm; arr thou; as it were, Vishnu hare O *Sarasvati*; O *Sinivali*, let her have progeny; may she be in the favor of Bhaga. Ath. 18.2.32.

Visvarupa is the son of Tvastr, is a three headed demon slain by both Trit and Indra.

Vivasvat is the father of the Aswin. 10.17.2, and of Yama 10.14.17.

Tvastr is described as ancestor of human race so far as his daughter Saranyu wife of *Vivasvat*, become the mother of the primeval twins *Yama and Yami*. Rg. 10.17.2, it has been said that *Tvastr* adorned all beings with forms known as omniform *Visvarupa*, who is son of *Tvastr*.

Sinivali is broad hipped, fair armed, fair fingered, prolific a mistress of a family, who grant progeny, she is invoked with Sarasvati, Raka as well as Gungu-Kuhu. Raka represents fool moon and Kuhu represents first day of moon. Rg. 2.32; 10.184

11
Origin of Life

Life on the earth is a chemical synthetic process of evolution A. I. Oparin 1922.

It is not a end of the problem but it opens a door for further research pertaining to the cycle of rebirth and death.

Energy transformation, growth and reproduction are the fundamental principles of life, which are common from the unicellular to multicullular organisms. All forms of life consist of cells and get originate from the preexisting cells only, they maintain their continuity through cell division. Which shows continuity of life principle, which became complex with the evolution. With the acceptance of the view that all the life forms have been originated from the preexisting cells only, it has given the importance to the quest as and when the first life was originated on the earth.

The various forms of the living beings are due to the difference in the base sequence of DNA (Deoxy ribose Nucleic Acid)and the number of the nucleotides in it. Otherwise all living beings have the same DNA as genetic material, which carries the hereditary characters from parents to the offsprings. The people of Vedic culture were fully acquainted with these facts about the life, they have described them in their own way in the vedic hymns.

About the origin of life, there are direct evidences in fhe Veda, they have indicated about the process of evolution, through which the creation has came in to the existence under space-time relationship.

The origin of life has been explained metaphorically in an anthropomorphic manner, they have revealed the fact that life on the earth has been generated through the process of chemical evolution, The first cell has been synthesized in the water, the same has been termed as celestial race under the name of *Ṛbhu*, from which the world of living beings came in to the existence.

With the synthesis of first living cell, how the system became selfsufficient and self regulated with the evolution, it has been explained through conversation in a symbolic fashion mataphorically.

a. Origin of the Cell

The first cell, which get synthesized in the sea water has been termed as Ṛbhu.

For the celestial Race this song of praise which gives wealth lavishly. Rg.1-20-1.

The celestial race, which has been praised here is *Ṛbhu*, who represents a mature cell, once a mature cell get synthesised in the nature it can maintain its continuity through the cell division, accordingly at the cellular level all the living organisms exhibits same functions in the nature. Hence the Ṛbhu has been described as the celestial race. How it came in to the existence it has been indicated symbolically, accordingly the first cell came in to the existence at its own, through energy transformation, as indicated by the sacrifice-*Yajna* (the actions and interactions). The *Indra*-Electricity is the first, who has appeared with its charges as indicated by the horse harnessed, with this the process of synthesis has beeb started. The *Nasatyas*-two charges, under temperature-pressure gradient brought a lightly rolling car, which signifies energy transformation in side a closed system in the early primitive conditions. They formed a nectar-yielding cow, it indicates about the anaerobic respiration. With their ability and actions they acquire the capacity for renewl, it indicates about the cell division. The gladdening drop (internal energy source) represents the life energy, which was get developed with the help of *Indra* (electricity), *Māruts* (water) and *Ādityas* (twelve *Āditya*), the sacrificial ladles (developing cell) was made new by *Tvastr* (DNA), it means first genetic material get synthesized in side the cell, it has given the capacity for division during primitive anaerobic conditions, in turn it was divided in to four, accordingly with time thrice seven fuels, which are five major elements, twelve *Āditya* (twelve months), three atmospheric layers and fundamental energy were in operation for its safety, in which every natural force was having its share. In this fashion the process of evolution being initiated with the formation of a prokaryotic cell and cell division.

Modern researches in the field of origin of life have demonstrated the abiotic formation of organic substances in the early prebiological history of the earth A.I. Oparin 1922, J.B.S. Haldane 1928 and Bungen Burg de Jong 1929, they have suggested that in the primitive conditions, coaservates may get produced, as and when two hydrophilic colloidal solutions carrying opposite charges are being mixed, the same has been expressed here as Gladdening drop (Life energy).

A.I. Oparin 1968 has also suggested that photosynthetic activity can be promoted, when porphyrin get incorporated in coaservates, the same has been indicated through a metaphor 'cow from skin' symbolically.

Rg. 1-20-2

1-2. They who for Indra, with their mind formed horses harnessed by a word. Attained by works to sacrifice.

3. They for Nasatyas (Aswin) wrought a light car moving every way: They formed a nectar yielding cow.

4. The Rbhus with effectual prayers, honest, with constant labour made. Their sire and mother young again.

5. Together came your gladdening drops with Indra by the Maruts girt. With the Adityas, with the Kings.

6. The sacrifice ladle, wrought newly by the God Twastar's hand— Four ladles have ye made thereof.

7. Vouchsafe us wealth, to him who pours thrice seven libations, ye to each. Give wealth, pleased with our eulogies.

8. As ministering Priests they held, by pious acts they won themsleves. A share in sacrifice with Gods.

Vedic knowledge on the Ṛbhu (Cell) is the testimony of the modern researches in the field of origin of life. Hence looking to its importance the hymns related with the Ṛbhu (cell) have been quoted here as references about Ṛbhu (cell) and Tvastar (DNA), which have been given at various places in the Ṛgveda.

Rg. 1.CX-The *Ṛbhus* (cells) have been praised foe their work and it has been said "O ye *Rbhus*, is this sea for all the Gods", it means for the natural forces the space in the cell is just like a vast ocean for their activity, which acts with the generation of magnetic life energy. The Soma represents magnetic life energy, which is being generated within the cell due to the movements of electrons in side a closed system. The same is the symbol of life in a cell, during the evolution at a certain stage, formation of the enzymes was has been indicated by the term Savita-stimulator. With this the cells have started dividing under natural conditions Rg. 1-CX-3, these were the children of *Sudhanvan* (developing cell), having a life of about a year and disappeared quickly in the atmosphere. Rg.1.CX-6. During the process of evolution, they have developed internal mode of nutrition under anaerobic conditions, which has been indicated by saying "they formed a cow, and brought the mother close unto her calf again," with this skill the aging cells became young, which has been indicated by saying "*Ṛbhus*, Ye made your aged parents youthful as before." Rg.1.CX-8. It means through the cell division, the cells became young, the daughter cells have been termed as young parents.

Ṛgveda 1.CX-1 to 8

1. The holy work I wrought before is wrought again: my sweetest hymn is sung to celebrate your praise. Here, O ye Rbhus, is this sea for all the Gods: sate you with Soma offered with the hallowing word.
2. When seeking your enjoyment onward from a far, ye came un to the home of liberal Savitar.

3. Savitar gave you immortality, because ye came proclaiming him whom naught can hide. And this the drinking- chalice of the Asura, which till that time was one, ye made to be fourfold.
4. When they had served with zeal at sacrifice as priests, they mortal as they were, gained immortality. The Ṛbhus, children of Sudhanvan, bright as suns were in a year's course made associate with prayers.
5. The Ṛbhus, with a rod measured, as were a field, the single sacrificial chalice wide of mouth.
6. As oil in ladles, we through knowledge will present un to the Heroes of the firmament our hymn.—The Ṛbhus who came near with this great Father's speed, and rose to heaven's high sphere to eat the strengthening food.
7. Ṛbhu to us is Indra freshest in his might, Ṛbhu with powers and wealth is giver of rich gifts. Gods, through your favor may we on the happy day quell the attacks of those who pour no offerings forth.
8. Out of skin, O Ṛbhus, once ye formed a cow, and brought the mother close un to her calf again. Sons of Sudhanvaṇ, Heroes, with surpassing skill ye made your aged parents youthful as before.

With working skill they wrought the lightly rolling car: they wrought the Bays (two charges) who bear Indra and bring great gifts.

The Ṛbhus for their parents made life young again; and fashioned for the calf a mother by its side. Rg. 1.CXI-1

The streaming movement of the charged particles has been indicated by lightly rolling car, which is a gift of nature. The electrical charges has been expressed through the bays who bear Indra.

The Ṛbhus for their parents made life young again; and fashioned for the calf a mother by its side. In the next stanza it has been said that "The *Ṛbhus* for their parents made life young again; and fashioned for the calf a mother by its side", the developing cells have been mentioned here as calf and its mother is a symbolic expression for the nourishment, who can nourish it. It indicates about the energy transformation in the primitive conditions, in turn the *Ṛbhus* (cells) have acquired longevity in the nature.

Rg. 1.CLIX-3. These sons of yours (Ṛbhus) well skilled in work of wondrous power, brought forth to life the two great mothers first of all.

To keep the truth of all that stands and all that moves, ye guard the station of your sons who knows know guile.

4. They with surpassing skill, most wise, have measured out the Twins united in their birth and in their home.

They refulgent Sages weave within the sky, ye in the depths of sea, a web for ever new. Rg. 1.CLIX-3, 4.

Here it has been indicated by the Vedic seers that during the evolution of life on the earth, The *Ṛbhus* (Cells) has acquired life through their skill of work, " brought the two great mothers first of all" it means oxidation and reduction reactions, which acts like two mothers through the synthesis of various products in the cell. They are the symbol of truth, it means through them the nature is working as a system, hence they have been termed as two mothers.Who regulates and feed the system through their byproducts.

With their skill they have synthesized a pair of twins, it means the two strips of the DNA base pairs. Which have brought webs of food chains in the sky and in the sea (world of living beings), which is always new.

It has been indicated here that the whole world of living beings have came in to existence from the genetic material DNA, which is a double helical structure. The same is responsible for the formation of food webs and food chains in the nature.

We get more information about the *Ṛbhu* (cell) in another hymn, where energy transformation has been praised, *Ṛbhus* came in to existence due to the Agni (energy), due to which the chalice (cup-cell) divided in to four and in turn the cells came in to the command of Gods (natural forces), through which they participate in the creation sacrifice. Rg. 1.CLXI-1, 2. It has been indicated here that through the energy transformation the developing cells have acquired the capacity for the division. The natural forces have influenced their further development. Accordingly with the actions and interactions, they became the part of the nature.

In the succeeding stanza symbolically the cell has been designated as chariot. For its easy run a need of a courser has been expressed, the courser is DNA, who has been expressed as *Tvastr*, simultaneously there was a question about the messenger. The courser of the cell is nucleus, who regulates the biochemical reactions. The messenger is DNA, who carries the message from one generation to another generation. It has been expressed that as soon as the cell has divided into four, the *Tvastr* (DNA), concealed him self in to the consorts of the gods (natural components). It means DNA get disappeared with the formation of the new cells. Rg. 1. CLXI-4, 5. In the nature, the genetic material is visible at the time of cell division and it disappears with the formation of the young cells. The same has been expressed here.

In the nature after cell division, the parent cell lost its identity and young cells take over their functions. Hence it has been said "let us slay these men, who reviled the chalice (parent cells)" and Rbhu made their parents young again with the new names.

For the further evolution Bays of *Indra*, electromagnetic energy carries it towards evolution, *Aswin* (morning and evening) have given it a further advancement. *The Brahaspati* (nucleus) brought the cow of every hue. It means through the regulation of the metabolic reactions various substances get synnthesised. Accordingly the cells have acquired different stages as *Ṛbhu*, *Vibhvan*, and *Vaja* during their life cycle. These three represents three stages of a cell as young, mature and old.

In the next step of evolution, the *Ṛbhus* (cells) have developed a self nourishment system, through the development of protochlorophyll in the primitive conditions, the same has been indicated through the 'Cow from the skin.' which acts as a horse and the cell became well equipped. It means in the primitive conditions, genetic material as

RNA or DNA first get synthesised in side a closed system, then with time protochlorophyll get synthesized from the cell wall, (In the primary conditions some compounds may have been deposited on the surface of the cells, which in turn may have given the way for the development of the cellwall and protochlorophyll with time). The synthesis of protochlorophyll with DNA have acted as a horsepower for the evolution, accordingly it has been said "Ye (Rbhu) brought a horse out of a horse." Thus the cell became resistant to survive in the nature through cell division, where DNA and chlorophyll have been termed as two horse. In the nature evolution of the living beings is due to the DNA and the development of the carbon skeleton is due to the chlorophyll through photosynthesis, which is the source of food for the living beings.

b. The Ecological and Physiological Principles

After describing the formation of a cell in the primitive conditions, how the nature is working as a system. It has been indicated through conversation in a anthropomorphic manner. Importance of the water for life has been indicated through "ye drink this water or ye drink water through rinsing of Munja grass", which indicates that animals drink water and plants (Munja grass) absorbs water through their root system. Accordingly water provides streaming capacity to the protoplasm and the life energy as well, the same has been indicated by the 'Gladdening drop', which is a metaphor for the life energy.

After indicating the importance of water, they have expressed the ecological and physiological functions in a symbolic fashion through conversation. Looking to the functions of the nature, according to the one water is important, the second one says that energy is important, the third one says that lightening clouds are important, the fourth one says that many factors are important. Than the Ṛbhu (cell) it self has revealed the truth through a riddle, about the basic principles under which the ecosystem is working as a system. The Ṛbhu (cell) has expressed the truth about respiration, photosynthesis and the decomposition of the dead parts, through which the system operates in the nature. "One downward to the water drives the crippled cow." The term 'crippled cow' has been used for the unwanted CO^2 (carbon dioxide), just like water moves in the downward direction in the same fashion carbon dioxide get released from the body. Which is unwanted in the body and as such get released during the respiration, but CO^2 is useful too for the photosynthesis and a source for the carbon skeleton of the living beings, hence the Vedic seers have used the term "crippled cow" for the carbon dioxide.

"Another trims the flesh brought on the carving board." Here the term 'flesh' has been used for the food material, which get synthesized during the photosynthesis in the cell (carving board), which get transported through the respiration and intermediary metabolism as food through living beings in the nature.

"One carries off the refuse at the set of sun." Here the term 'set of sun' has been used for the end of life symbolically. The dead parts under go decomposition through microbes in the nature, in turn waste material get released from the surface, these principles have given the way for the evolution of the living beings. Hence degradation and decomposition of the waste material by the decomposers has been indicated.

These three important ecological and physiological functions are going on in the nature, through which the nature is working as an ecosystem. Looking towards the ecosystem a question has been asked "how did the parents aid their children in their task". The parents here represents preexisting living beings. The answer has been given through the grass for man and water in the valley. Through this biogeochemacal cycle has been indicated. It means the preexisting living beings are the source of nourishment for the ecosystem, through the development of the soil system. Where after the death the dead parts get converted in to the organic manure and water initiates the growth of the grasses.

The work of *Ṛbhu* (cell) due to which the creation system came in to existence is not for once only but it is repeated due to the fact that "he is sleeping in the house of him whom nothing can hide", it means life energy gets generated at its own, through the preexisting cells.

Rg. 1.CLXI

1. Working skill they wrought the lightly rolling car: they wrought the Bays (life and death), who bear Indra and bring great gifts.
2. The Rbhus for their Parents made life young again; and fashioned for the calf a mother by its side.

   The chalice that is single make ye in to four : thus have the Gods commanded; therefore am I come.

   If O Sudhanvan's Children, ye will do this thing, ye shall participate in sacrifice with Gods.
3. What to the envoy Agni in reply ye spoke, A courser must be made, a chariot fashioned here. A cow must be created, and the Twain made young. When we have done these things, brother, we turn to you.
4. When thus O Ṛbhus, ye had done ye questioned thus Whither went he who came to us a messenger?

   Then Tvastar, when he viewed the for wrought chalices, concealed him self among the Consorts of the Gods.
5. As Tvastar thus had spoken, let us slay these men who have reviled chalice, drinking cup of gods. They gave themselves new names when Soma juice was shed, and under these new names the Maiden welcomed them.
6. Indra hath yoked his Bays, the Asvin's car is horsed, Brahaspati hath brought the Cow of every hue. Ye went as Ṛbhu, Vibhvan, Vaja to the Gods.
7. Ye by your wisdom brought a cow from out a hide; un to that ancient Pair ye gave again their youth. Out of a horse, Sudhanvan's Sons, ye formed a horse: a chariot ye equipped and went un to the Gods.
8. Drunk ye this water, were the words ye spake to them; or drink ye this, the rinsing of the Munja-grass. If ye approve not even this, Sudhanvan's Sons, then at the third libation gladden ye yourselves.
9. Most excellent are waters, thus said one of you; most excellent is Agni, thus another said.

Another praised to many a one the lightening cloud. Then did ye shape the cups, speaking the words of truth.

10. One downward to the water drives the crippled cow, another trims the flesh brought on the carving board.

One carries off the refuse at the set of sun. How did the Parents aid their children in their task.

11. On the high places ye have made the grass for man, and water in the valleys, by your skill, O Men. Ṛbhus, ye iterate not today that act of yours, you are sleeping in the house of him whom naught can hide. See Rg. vol. 4 also.

Hymn XXXIII Ṛbhus

1. I send my voice as herald to the Ṛbhus; I crave the white cow for the overspreading,

   Wind-sped, the Skilful Ones in rapid motion have in an instant compassed round the heaven.

2. What time the Ṛbhus had with care and marvels done proper service to assist their Parents,

   They won the friendship of the Gods; the Sages carried away the fruit of their devotion.

3. May they who made their Parents, who were lying like posts that moulder, young again for ever,

   May Vaja, Vibhvan, Ṛbhu, joined with Indra, protect our sacrifice, the Soma-lovers.

4. As for a year the Ṛbhus kept the Milch-cow, throughout a year fashioned and formed her body,

   And through a year's space still sustained her brightness, through these their labours they were made immortal.

5. Two beakers let us make,-thus said the eldest. Let us make three,-this was the younger's sentence,

   Four beakers let us make,-thus spoke the youngest. Tvastar approved this rede of yours, O Ṛbhus.

6. The men spake truth and even so they acted : this Godlike way of theirs the Ṛbhus followed,

   And Tvastar, when he looked on the four beakers resplendent as the day, was moved with envy.

7. When for twelve days the Ṛbhus joyed reposing as guests of him who never may be hidden,

They made fair fertile fields, they brought the rivers. Piants spread o'er deserts, waters filled the hollows.

8. May they who formed the swift car, bearing Heroes, and the Cow omniform and all-impelling,

   Even may they form wealth for us,-the Ṛbhus, dexterous-handed, deft in work and gracious.

9. So in their work the Gods had satisfaction, pondering it with thought and mental insight,

   The Gods' expert artificer was Vaja, Indra's Rbhuksan, Varuna's was Vibhvan.

10. They who, made glad with sacrifice and praises, wrought the two Bays, his docile Steeds, for Indra,

    Ṛbhus, as those who wish a friend to prosper, bestow upon us gear and growth of riches.

11. This day have they set gladdening drink before you. Not without toil are Gods inclined to friendship,

    Therefore do ye who are so great, O Ṛbhus, vouchsafe us treasures at this third libation.

Hymn XXXIV Ṛbhus

1. To this our sacrifice come Ṛbhu, Vibhvan, Vaja, and Indra with the gift of riches, Because this day hath Dhisana the Goddess set drink for you : the gladdening draughts have reached you.

2. Knowing your birth and rich in gathered treasure, Ṛbhus, rejoice together with the Rtus,

   The gladdening draughts and wisdom have approached you: send ye us riches with good store of heroues.

3. For you was made this sacrifice, O Ṛbhus, which ye, like men, won for yourselves aforctime,

   To you come all who find in you their pleasure : ye all were-even the two elder-Vajas.

4. Now for the mortal worshipper, O Heroes, for hime who served you, was the gift of riches,

   Drink, Vajas, Ṛbhus ! unto you is offered, to gladden you, the third and great libation.

5. Come to us, Heroes, Vajas and Rbhuk-sans, glorified for the sake of mighty treasure,

These draughts approach you as the day is closing, as cows, whose calves are newly-born, their stable.

6. Come to this sacrifice of ours, ye Children of Strength, invoked with humble adoration,

   Drink of this meath, Wealth-givers, joined with Indra with whom ye are in full accoud, ye Princes.

7. Close knit with Varuna drink the Soma, Indra; close-knit, Hymn-lover ! with the Maruts drink it,

   Close-knit with drinkers first, who drink in season; close-knit with heavenly Dames who give us treasures.

8. Rejoice in full accord with the Adityas, in concord with the Parvatas, O Ṛbhus; In full accord with Savitar, Divine One; in full accord with floods that pour forth riches.

2. Knowing your birth : knowing how you have attained immortality and deification. The Rtvs : the seasons personified and honoured as deities. The Ṛbhus as cosmic powers are closely connected with them.

3. Vajas : the is, although Vaja is strictly the name of the youngest of the three only, you are all entitled to that appellation which means active, strong, or spirited. Professor Grassmann translates: 'ihr alle seid die ersten hier, ? Vadscha's;' ye are all the first (entitled to precedence) here, ? V jas; but the word uta is then left untranslated.

4. The third and great libation : see the preceding hymn, stanza II.

5. Ṛbhuksans : Ṛbhuksan is another name of Ṛbhu, the eldest of the three.

7. Drinkers first : those who claim and receive the libation first; here, apparently, the Ṛtus or Seasons.

8. Parvatas : Gods presiding ever mountains and clouds.

9. Ṛbhus, who helped their Parents and the Asvins, who formed the Milch-cow and the pair of horses,

   Made armour, set the heaven and earth asunder,-far-reaching Heroes, they have made good offspring.

10. Ye who have wealth in cattle and in booty, in heroes, in rich sustenance and treasure,

    Such, O ye Ṛbhus, first to drink, rejoicing, give unto us and those who laud our present.

11. Ye were not for : we have not left you thirsting, blameless in this our sacrifice, O Ṛbhus,

Rejoice you with the Maruts and with Indra, with the Kings, Gods ! that ye may give us riches.

Rg. Volume 4. XXXV

1. Come hither, O ye Sons of Strength, ye Ṛbhus; stay not afar, ye Children of Sudhavan,

   At this libation is your gift of treasure. Let gladdening drop approach you after Indra's.

2. Hther is come the Ṛbhu's gift of riches; here was the drinking of the well - Soma. Pressed Soma,

   Since by dexterity and skill as craftsman ye made the single chalice to be fourfold.

3. Ye made fourfold the chalice that was single: ye spake these words and said O Friend, assist us;

   Then Vajas! gained the path of life eternal, deft handed Ṛbhus, to the God's assembly.

4. Out of what substance was that chalice fashioned which ye made fourfold by your art and wisdom?

5. Ye with your cunning made your parents youthful; the cup, for Gods to drink ye formed with cunning;

   With cunning, Ṛbhu rich in treasure fashioned the two swift Twany Steeds who carry Indra.

6. Whoso pours out for you, when days are closing, the sharp libation for your joy, O Vajas,

   For him O mighty Ṛbhus, ye rejoicing have fashioned wealth with plenteous store of heroes.

7. Lord of Bay Steeds, at dawn the juice thou drankest: thine, only thine, is the noon- day libation,

   Now drink thou with the wealth bestowing Rbhus, whom for thir skill thou madest friends, O Indra.

8. Ye whom your artist skill hath raised to God head have set you down above in heaven like falcons,

   So give us riches, Children Sudhanvan, O Sons of Strength; ye have become immortal.

9. The third libation, that bestoweth treasure which ye have won by skill, ye dexterous- handed,

   This drink hath been effused for you, Ṛbhus: drink it with high delight, with joy like Indras.

Rg. 4. XXXIII. 5, 6.

Rg.4. XXXV. 2, 3, 4

Rg.4. XXXVI. 3, 4

To express the concern knowledge riddles are a important tool in the Veda, the two riddles, which are related with life are as under - Rg. 10-LXXIX-1. I have beheld the might of this Great Being. Immortal in the midst of tribes of mortals.(Life energy in a cells)

2. His eyes are turned away, his head is hidden: unsated with his tounge he eats the fuel. (cell metabolism has been indicated)

Conclusion—Origin of Life

It seems that the fundamental energy is the original source of the creation, from where the different components of the nature have been synthesized, through energy transformation under temperature—pressure gradient. The first cell has been synthesized in the water at its own under natural conditions, with energy transformation in side a closed system. It has acquired life energy, this energy can be generated due to the movements of the charged particles in side a closed system. This energy is the first symbol of the life, with the evolution of the living beings in the nature, the life energy is also having its evolution. Which gradually attains stability in the young cells with metabolic reactions and under go gradually towards its end through aging of the cells.

The life energy is a form of the fundamental energy. With the evolution of the multi cellular organisms, the life energy is having a common appearance. The evolution of the living beings and their various forms are due to the evolution of the DNA base sequence with the complexity of genetic code. Which carries the hereditary characters from one generation to another generation. In this way DNA in one direction regulates the course of life through hereditary characters in the living beings, and on the another side streaming of the protoplasm in the living cells provides it life energy with metabolic reactions as its food. Which gets further strength through the movement of the sap in the plants and circulation of the blood in the animals. In human beings and in the higher animals, it gets further strength with the evolution through the development of the nervous system, Their movements and metabolic functions in the body enhance the production of life energy. Which are its stimulators, because they generate magnetic energy during their ciculatory movements, which undergo deterioration with aging and ultimately life energy get seized with the inactivity of the concern organs. In this way there are two centers in the body one is DNA and other is life energy, both are important for the life and independent for their functions but present simultaneously at one place with having a common purpose of life in the living beings.

The same has been indicated by the Vedic seers through a metaphor in *Ṛgveda* and *Upanishads.* Two birds with fair wings, knit with bonds of friendship, in the same sheltering tree have found refuge.

One of the twins eats the sweet Fig-tree's fruitage; the other eating not regardeth only.

On this stanza Sayana says that the two birds are the vital and the supreme spirit, dwelling in one body. The vital spirit enjoys the fruit or rewards of actions while the supreme spirit is merely a spectator. Rg. 1.164.20.

Through the example of two birds on the same tree, out of which one enjoy the sweet fruit and other one is only a spectator. Here the Vedic seers have indicated about the existence of the DNA in the body, who through its hereditary characters leads the life in the body with its actions, through protein synthesis and regulates the life. The same has been termed as *Jeewatma–bio soul*, and the other one is life driving energy, which is in no way different from the fundamental energy, the same is the supreme spirit in the body as spectator, commonly known as soul. Accordingly the soul in the body and the fundamental energy (*God*) are one and the same. Hence in the Upnishads it has been said that "*Atma so Parmatma*" means the God and soul are one. It is *Jeewatma*-bio soul (DNA) , who bears the pains of life. Which is immortal in the sense that it has maintained its continuity in the living beings and remains active through its offsprings. Hence the DNA is the same from the unicellular to multicellular organisms.

The existence of the self generated life energy has been indicated through a metaohor.

The lotus flower of nine doors, covered with three strands (guna)-what soulful prodigy (yaksha) is within it, that the Brahaman knowers know.

The lotus flower of nine doors, it signifies human body with three qualities growth, reproduction and energy transformation. The presence of life energy has been indicated through Yaksa. Ath. 10.8

Free from desire, wise (dhira), immortal, self existent, satisfied with sap, not deficient in any respect-knowing that wise, unaging young soul, one is not afraid of death. Ath. 10.8

The presence of life energy has been expressed that life energy is self existent, without desire, eternal, satisfied with the sap. It means the life energy gets generated at its own, through the streaming of the sap.

12
Photosynthesis in the Wedding Hymns

The photosynthesis is a process, during which the green plants synthesise glucose as food material from the atmospheric carbon di oxide and water in the presence of chlorophyll and light. During this prosess the transformation of the light energy in to the chemical energy is there, which is the source of life and food for the living organisms. Today it is also a fact that all the complex organic substances are the products of the glucose metabolism in side the cell. It is a unique event in the history of origin of life on the earth. Which is the only source of the chemical energy and carbon skeleton of the living beings on the earth.

The process of the photosynthesis has been described, through the metaphor of the marriage ceremony in the wedding hymns of the Rgveda and Atharvaveda.

The sun's wheel is its bridal car on which the sun is coming to give his daughter to her husband. The seven visible rays are the seven sisters and *Narsams* is her younger sister. It means short blue wavelength of light . The *Aryaman* is long red wavelength of light, which are important for the photolysis of water and conversion of the light energy in to the chemical energy. The husband's house is a cell ,where she is going to enter as a wife to unite with her husband (CO^2), so as to form a union with her husband (glucose). Which is the source of offsprings (products). The house where she is going to produce progeny is guarded by *the Soma*-magnetic energy, *Mitra*-light, *Varuna*-gravity and *the Indra*-electrical energy. *Tvastr*-The DNA help her to produce

Visvarupa-(The various forms of the living beings) Rg.10.85, (*Atharvaveda 14.1 and* 2).The importance of the chlorophyll has been discussed under the name of *Avi*-protector and *Parna mani in the Ath*arvaveda., In the Rigveda its presence has been indicated under the name of Bhragu.

The deity, *Avi* by name, sits enveloped with right; by her form these trees are green garlanded. Ath. X.8.31

As twere some goodly treasure *Matrisvan* brought as a gift to *Bhrgu.* Rg. 1.LX.1

The Matrisvan (CO^2) has brought down from heaven to earth, which is a gift to Bragu (chlorophyll), it means the gift is for photosynthesis.

It reflects about the knowledge and importance of the chlorophyll and the carbon dioxide for the living beings.

Marriage ceremony is a unique event in the life of a human being, through marriage a young girl under go a transformation. She enters in to a new house as a wife with her husband so as to produce offsprings. In the same way transformation of the light energy in to the chemical energy through photosynthesis lead it to produce glucose and the products of the glucoseare its offsprings. Through the ceremonial process and the wedding hymns of the marriage, the whole process of the photosynthesis has been described in a symbolic fashion, which is miraculously same as we know today, through the achievements of the modern science in the field of Biophysics.

The wedding hymn start with the indication that under the cosmic principles the soma is set in the sky, due to the soma sun has been established in the sky, due to the soma the *Ādityas* are strong and earth is mighty; like wise in the midst of asterism soma has been placed. It has been also indicated here that soma is not a plant or moon but an energy, which no one ever tastes. The soma represents magnetic energy, According to the priciples of modern Astronomy. The magnetic energy can be generated due to the movements of the electrons in side a atom and in all the

Astronomical bodies, who are moving at their axis, as due to the movement at their axis, a dynamo is being developed in their center. Due to this all rotating Astronomical bodies have their own magnetic field and the magnetosphere around them. The position and the importance of the sun, earth and other planets in the universe is due to their magnetic field and the magnetosphere. The inter planetary space is filled with the inter planetary magnetic field, along with this due to the movements of electrons around the nucleus in a atom magnetic energy gets generated. Which get associated with the electrostatic energy of the nucleus and produces the bond energy, which binds the atoms and molecules in the various substances. In the living beings due to the streaming movements of the protoplasm, the magnetic energy gets generated, which is responsible for the origin of life. Hence it has been expressed that soma (magnetic energy) is present every where, which indicates about the presence of the fundamental energy (Soma). Accordingly in the wedding hymn first of all soma has been appreciated, it has been said that soma is the bride seeker, it is due to the presence of soma in the living cells, which is also the house in which the sun's light energy is going to enter for the transformation. Ath. XIV.1.9.

When, *Sūrya* went to her husband, here the wheel of the sun is its bridal car. Ath. XIV.1.61. The solar flares have been described as *the Surya's* excellent garment, as and when the solar wind passes through the sky, the high energetic solar wind waves makes noise. The movement of the solar particles looks like that as if they are dancing. Vedic seers have expressed the same through *raibhe* and *Gatha.* The Narasa*m*sa is her younger sister, it means a short blue wavelength of light Rg. 10.85.6. Ath. XIV.1.7. *Aryaman* is long red wavelenth of light, who is husband finder bride Ath. XIV.1.17.

Bridesmen, *Asvin* represents rising and setting sun, *Agni* -heat energy has been described as fore runner, *Savitar* is stimulator. It means with changes in temperature-pressure gradient, it stimulates the process. When *the Surya* approaches her husband's home, his two draft oxen were white. It is the indication of the white visible light, as and when the sun rays reaches on the earth they have white colour. Ath. XIV.1.9 & 10.

During the cource of the sun light from the sky to the earth, the Ultra Violet rays are get absorbed by the ozone layer in the upper atmosphere. This fact has been indicated through asking a question to *Aswin* "with your three wheeled chariot, to *Sūrya's* bridal. Where was one wheel of yours" Ath. XIV.1.14,16

"The two wheels of thee, O *Sūrya*, the priests know, the one wheel that is in secret-that verily, the enlightened know."

The course of the solar rays from the sky to earth is being completed in three steps, which have been designated here as three wheels. The first step is in the sky, where sun rays gets generated due to the nuclear reactions at the surface of the sun, the second step is sun's visible light on the earth's surface. These are the two common steps, the third invisible step is in the atmosphere, where ozone layer absorbs the toxic Ultra Violet rays. The same has been indicated as the one wheel that is in secret.

a. Light Reaction

The photosynthesis has two main reactions, the light reaction and dark reaction.It is during the light reaction that the sun light (long red wavelength of light) gets converted in to the chemical energy with the help of chlorophyll (photosynthetic pigments). Here *Bhag* represents photosynthetic pigment, which leads the *Aryaman* (long red wavelength of light) for the union. The place where the light energy is going to enter is the cell. Here it has been addressed to the light energy that "watch thou over this house in order to housewife ship ; mingle thy self with this husband for thy progeny" Ath. XIV.1.21. Here the light energy (long red wave length of light) is bride and carbon di oxide is bridegroom, addressing to them it has been said that "ye (two) just here; be not separated; attain your whole life- time sporting with sons and grand sons" Ath.

XIV.1.22. The sons and grand sons are symbolic expressions for the products of the glucose, in the same sequence again it has been said that "these two move one after the other by magic these two sporting young ones" Ath. XIV.1.23, 24. Here in a symbolic manner anabolic and catabolic reactions have been indicated, by saying that by their own power these Twain in close succession move; they go as playing children round the sacrifice (actions and interactions in a cyclic manner) Rg. 10.LXXXV.18a. It means these two reactions operate in succession one after the other.

"One of the pair beholdeth all existing things; the other ordereth seasons and is born again" Rg.10.LXXXV.18b. One holds all existing things. Here it has been indicated that the existence of the living beings in the creation is due the chemical energy and the other one is the product of the photosynthesis (glucose), which under go oxidation and due to the biochemical reactions under the seasonal variations, it acquires different forms and shapes again and again. It indicates about the formation of the different substrates from the glucose molecule. Addressing to the glucose again it has been said that with its formation it became new and new from morning to evening and disposes shares of Gods (natural components), it means the glucose is the source of thedifferent organic substances, which reaches to their respective places as food, as indicated through moon, which represent night, which extends the length of man's existence. Rg. 10.LXXXV.19, Ath. IV.1.24. It means night is the proper time for the transportation of the food material, which extend the longevity of the human beings.

b. Electron Transfer

During the light reaction chlorophyll molecules absorbs photons (quanta) and become excited. It means the molecules with more energy than the ground state energy. The excess energy absorbed by the chlorophyll molecule is passed on to one of its electron, which is consequently raised to a higher energy level. The high energy electron is than expelled from the chlorophyll with excess energy, such electron have a very short life. If they do not immediately participate in the photochemical reactionthey. than they loss their energy partly as heat and partly as radiation as fluorescence or phosphorescence (energy transfer in steps). As a result due to the loss of some of the energy as heat the electron will fall to meta triplet state. It is these activated triplet state electrons by virtue of their longer life, they can most easily be involved in the photochemical reaction known as photo phosphorylation and the electron will return to the ground state.During this journey of the electron it losses its excess energy thrice, first from the excited singlet state to the 2nd excited singlet state. This state can also be obtained by the absorption of blue light but such electrons have very short life. Again it losses its energy as heat to give electrons at the first excited singlet state, this state can also be obtained when chlorophyll absorbs red light. Such electrons are also short lived and under go internal conversion to meta triplet state and get involved in the photochemical reaction. Up to this state the excited electrons losses the excess energy thrice hence Vedic seers have termed it as thrice purified.The excess energy has been indicated through a metaphor of a garment which has been infected by the witchcraft, so it has been said that before entering the house as a wife give away garment *(Camulya)*. The importance of the blue and red light have been indicated by saying that it become blue-red when witchcraft's infection get driven away.

It means excited electron loss some of its energy as heat and become blue- red, which is 2nd excited and 1st excited state of the electron respectively.

If the husband wraps his body with *camulya* then his body becomes unpleasent. It means excited electrons with excess energy are harmful, the sun rays are having different wavelengths of light, they get released their excess energy in parts through phosphorescence, Ath. XIV.1.28. The high intensity of light is like a harsh barbed poison, the priest *brahma* who know *Surya*, he indeed deserves the brides garment, who verily takes the garment and bride remains un harmed. Ath. XIV.1.29, 30.

It has been indicated here that excess energy-*camulya*, when released in the steps then the released energy get accepted by *the brahma*-ADP and ATP (Adenosine tri Phosphate) get synthesized through the photophosphorylation, which is associated with the pigment system Ist and excited electrons move to the pigmant system-IInd.

The importance of the chemical energy has been expressed in the succeeding stanza, it has been prayed to the Brahamanaspati (nucleus) that the chemical energy with her husband (glucose), the two may proceed on a successful path and the glucose may shine for the chemical energy as carbon products and it has been prayed that the environmental factors may favour him on her path.

By saying that "now I remove the glistening seizor, body spoiling; that I draw up". Ath. XIV-1-38. It means that now the excited electrons are ready for the biochemical reaction. For the light reaction the water molecule is having a important role, its importance has been expressed in this fashion. "He who shines without fuel within the waters, whom the devout praise at the sacrifices (*Adhvara*). O child of the waters, mayest thou give waters rich in honey, with which *Indra* increased, full heroism". Ath. XIV-1-37. In this verse latent energy of the water has been indicated. The *Indra* represents the electricity, the electric energy with its two charges help in the *Photolysis* of water (H+ + OH-). In the nature with this the exited chlorophyll molecule of the pigment system 2nd reached to the ground state by receiving the electron from the water through photolysis, which has been expressed as the heroic act of the Indra (the electricity). In the nature it is related with the short blue wavelength of light and the noncyclic photophosphorylation, then the electrons get moves to Ist exited state. Which is the seat of the long red wavelength of light. The fact has been indicated by saying "Let the *Brahamin* take for her (water) for bathing; let them draw waters that slay not a hero; let her go about the fire of *Aryaman* (long red wave length of light)", here the photolysis of the water has been indicated and then the electrons get moved towards the next state, the same is the fire of *Aryaman* and the *Metatriplet* state, from where a biochemical reaction start. The same has been described as *"O thou of hundred activities, having thrice purified Apala"*, (Up to this state the excited electrons have released their energy through phosphorescence thrice, hence the excited electrons are thrice purified.. As suggested by Arnon 1954 "O *Indra*, thou didst make her sun skinned", the term 'sun skinned' has been used for the chemical energy and has been expressed in the next verse that "becoming obedient to thy husband, gird thy self in order to immortality". With the formation of the glucose molecule the chemical energy acquire different forms and remains active as immortal The immortal nature of the chemical energy has been expressed. Through the anabolic and catabolic reactions in the living beings. It moves in to the food chains and food webs in the nature and remains active as immortal. The glucose is the primary source of the food material, which is the source of complex carbon skeleton of all the living beings. Which form a complex food webs and food chains in the ecosystem, the same has been indicated through a question that "They who spun, wove and who stretched the web, what divine one gave the ends about, let them wrap thee in order to old age one long lived put this garment (glucose)." Ath. XIV.1.45. Rg.10.130.1. In a symbolic way the indication about the anabolic and catabolic reactions have been given. They are the architect of the complex food chains and food webs in the nature. The same has been expressed in the Athrvaveda.The food web is being generated due to the oxidation and reduction reactions in the nature, which operates simultaneously, which move one after the another, which one is first one can'nt say. Atharvaveda X.7.42, 43, 44.

c. Dark Reaction

In this way first the transformation of energy has been expressed "This is that form in which young woman (A particular wavelength of light) dressed her self; I desire to know with my mind the wife moving about; I will go after her with nine fold comrades; who, knowing unloosened these fetters." Ath. XIV.1.56. The reduction of the carbon di oxide through the Calvin cycle has been indicated. The nine comrades represents the nine products of the dark reaction. In Rigveda it has been expressed through "Ten sons and a husband (glucose) as a eleventh man" Rg. 10.LXXXV.45 (As suggested by Melvin Calvin 1946, 1951)

The first organic molecule glucose has been considered as a husband of the chemical energy. The chemical energy has entered in to the cell through transformation and present in the glucose as free energy, the chemical energy has been termed as the household wife (the chemical energy). This woman has received garment for beauty from *Tvastr* (the DNA) by the direction of *the Brahaspati*(regulator of the metabolic reactions in the cell) "*Savitar* and *Bhag* has enveloped this woman, like *Surya* with progeny" means- *Bhag* (Photosynthetic pigment) and *Savitar* has accepted it, as *Savitar* (enzymes) stimulates it so as to produce progeny, it means different products of the glucose molecule, which get synthesised in side a cell), the regulator of the synthesis is nucleus (Brahaspati) and the various products like the carbohydrates, fats and proteins are the products of the same glucose molecule under the guidence of the DNA (Deoxy Ribose Nucleic Acid), hence it has been said that the woman has received garment for the beauty from the Tvastr (DNA). Ath. XIV.1.53.

The factors, which influence the photosynthesis have been indicated as *Indra-Soma*-electriomagnetic energy, *Matriswan* (CO^2), *Mitra* (light) *Varun* (gravity), *Bhag* (photosynthetic pigments). Aswin (morning & evening), it is the indication about the importance of the light intensity, which under go a change from the morning to the the evening, *Maruts* (Water clouds), *Brahamin* (Soma-magnetic energy in the cell). These factors initiates and control the process Ath. XIV.1.54.

$6CO^2 + 6H_2O \rightarrow Light + Chlorophyll = Glucose + 6O2$

Further it has been said that "*Bhag* has fashioned four feet, *Bhag* has fashioned the four frames and *Tvastr* adorned the straps". Ath. XIV-1-60. Here it has been indicated that during the synthesis of the glucose it has four steps, these four steps represents the carbon dioxide (CO^2), Water (H_2O), Glucose ($C6H1_2O_6$) and Oxygen (O_2), they under go oxidation-reduction reactions and stimulates the process of the synthesis, the four frames-pieces represents four base pairs on the DNA strips. the DNA *(Tvastr)* is a genetic material with four base pairs, which regulates the protein synthesis and the course of life of the living beings.

In this way a all formed bridal car (Cell) get established on the journey of the cell towards the evolution. The DNA strips are the two pillars on the natural path-God made road, in the end of the hymn presence of the fundamental energy every where has been expressed under the name of *Brahamin.* Ath. XIV.1.64.

In the wedding hymns it has been said about the bride (sun rays) "Soma's wife first; the *Gandharva* thy next husband; *Agni* is thy third husband; thy fourth, one of human birth, accordingly Soma gave it to *Gandharva* and *Gandharva* gave it to *Agni* with wealth and son, Agni has given it to to me like wise this woman".Ath. XV.2.3, 4. Here in a symbolic fashion the journey of the light rays after the transformation has been indicated, as soon as the light energy approaches the cell, first it get received by the Soma, which is present in the cell due to the streaming of the protoplamic in side a cell, Soma gave it to *Gandharva* (protoplasm), it means than the energy enter in to the protoplasm, than it under go the biochemical reactions, hence it has been said that *Gandharva* gave it to *Agni*-metabolic energy, accordingly the various substances are get synthesized inside a cell. The products have been described as wealth and in the succession with the evolution human birth is there, like wise this woman *Agni* has given to me. Ath. XV.2.3, 4. It means through the material wealth of the photosynthetic food material, the human beings came in to the existence and likewise this woman also. It is a indication towards the organic evolution.

"O ye (two) of abundant good things, O *Aswin*; ye have been twin keepers, lord of beauty we, being dear, attain favorers (*Aryaman*) of our homes." Here two of abundant good things are morning and evening, who favour the Aryaman for the photosynthesis. It means that morning and evening hours are important, which favor the photosynthesis.

"Prey hear ye now of me, O men, by what blessings (acts) the two spouses attain what is agreeable (*vama*): what *Gandharvas* (there are) and heavenly *Apsarases*, who stand upon these forest trees (*vanaspatya*), let them be pleasant un to this bride; let them not injure the bridal car as it is driven". Here the two spouses represents anbolism and catabolism, *Gandharva* represents protoplasm and the heavenly *Apsarases* are the indicators of the cyclic metabolic reactions, which if uninjured leads to the evolution and accordingly the indications about the probable obstructions have been given, during the journey of the chemical energy from the green cell to its destiny in the nature. With the formation of a well equipped (well developed eukaryotic cell) a vast field is get open for the evolution the same has been indicated in Ath. XV.2.14. Further it has been indicated that from this plants and animals of various forms have been born. Ath. XV.2.22, 25.

"The gold cushioned vehicle, bearing all forms, did *Surya*, *Savitar's* daughter, mount, in order to great good progeny"(well developed cell) Ath. XV.2.30. The gods in the beginning lay with (*ni-pad*) their spouses; they embraced (*sam*-prac) bodies;(indication of crossing over) like *Surya*, O woman, all formed, with greatness, having progeny, unite (*sam-bhu*) here with thy husband." Ath. XV.2.32. Accordingly the functions of a mature cell have been expressed symbolically, through the family relationships universal importance of the chemical energy and the carbon has been indicated.

d. The wedding hymns—Conclusion

In the wedding hymn, if we are acquainted with the Vedic terminology than we can interpret the symbolic expression about the process of photosynthesis. The wheel of the sun is *surya's* bridal car. *Narsams* is the short blue wavelength of light and *Aryaman*-the long red wavelength of light. *Bhag* is the photosynthetic pigment, *Aswin* is a pair of morning and evening, Savitar is stimulator, who stimulate the light rays through change in temperature pressure gradient as well as it represents enzymes, who stimulates biochemical reactions. *Aryaman* is bride, *Bhag* is the pigment of the cell, where the long red wavelength of lighti is going to enter as a wife, Soma is bride seeker. During the transformation, the light energy under go purification through release of energy, as soon as it enter in to the system, the high energetic rays are toxic, which have been expressed through witchcraft's infection and harsh, sharp barbed poison, when its energy gets lower down it became blue-red than it enter in to the third step. When it approaches finally for the transformation, it releases its excess energy thrice, hence the light energy has been termed as thrice purified (*Apala*) at the Metatriplet state of the exited electrons. Importance of the water has been expressed through the water for bathing for bride, After the transformation as soon as the chemical energy gets generated, it is said that *Bhag* has grasped thy hand and *Savitar* has grasped thy hand means the pigments and the enzymes have accepted you and her husband is glucose, *Tvastar* (DNA) has given garment for the beauty, it means synthesis of protein, through which it acquires different forms and shapes.

During the process *Indra*, *Agni* (Electromagnetic energy), heaven and earth, *Matariswan* (Co_2), *Mitra* (light), *Varun* (gravity), *Maruts* (Water clouds), *Bhag* (the pigment), *Aswin* (morning-evening) and *Brahaspati* (nucleus). These are the factors, which control the photosynthesis. Indication towards the reduction of the carbon di oxide has been given through ten intermediate products as ten sons and glucose as a eleventh man.

Bhag has fashioned the four feet, these are the four steps during the process of photosynthesis, which involve the carbon dioxide Co_2, water and the synthesis of glucose with release of oxygen O_2. *Bhag* has fashioned the four frames-pieces and *Tvastar* adorned the straps, it indicates about the formation of the DNA base pairs with four bases (Adenine=Thyminme, Guanine≡Cytosine, Thymine=Adenine and Cytosine≡=Guanine.). "On the God made road (natural path) this bridal car is well flowered," it means it is a self sufficient system, where the transcription and translation are the two pillars on her natural path. The same has been expressed as a maiden and -two pillars. In the end of the wedding hymn it has been expressed that all Gods (the natural forces) have united us of one accord by heart, *Apah* (Water), *Matriswan* (CO_2), *Dhata* (sun) and *Saraswati* (*Vak*-universe) may unite us. Here it has been indicated that during the process of the photosynthesis Water, carbon di oxide and sun rays are important, which has given the way for the union (glucose), where carbon di oxide gets converted in to the glucose with chemical energy within it.

Through the wedding it has been indicated that the glucose with the chemical energy within it is the primary source of the carbon skeleton and the evolution of the living beings on the earth.

References from Atharvaveda on Photosynthesis Wedding hymns and Genetics Funeral hymns Book XIV-1-2 Translation by Whitney

Marriage Ceremonies

1. By truth is the earth established (ut-stabh) ; by the sun is the sky established ; by righteousness the Adiyas stand; Soma is set (crita) upon the sky.
2. By Soma are the Adityas strong ; by Soma is the earth great; likewise in the lap of these asterisms is Soma placed (a-dha).
3. One thinks himself to have drunk Soma when they crush up an herb ; what Soma the priests (brahman) know, of that no earthly man partakes.

4. When, O Soma, they drink thee (up), then thou fillest thyself up again ; Vayu is Soma's defender ; the month is norm (akrti) of the years (sama).
5. Guarded by covering-arrangements, defended by watchmen (?? barhata), O Soma, thou standest hearing the pressing-stones; no earthly one partakes of thee.
6. Intention (citti) was the pillow, sight was the ointment, heaven [and] earth were the coffer (koca), when Surya went to her husband.
7. The raibhi was the parting [song] (?? Anudeyi), the naracansi was the welcoming one (? Nyocani) ; Surya's garment verily was excellent ; she goes adorned with song (gatha).
8. The laudations (stoma) were the cross-pieces (?? Pratidhi) ; meter was the kurira, the opaca ; of Surya the Acvins were the wooers, Agni was the forerunner.
9. Soma was the bride-seeker ; both Acvins were wooers, when Savitar gave to her husband Surya, praising (cans) with her mind.
10. Mind was her cart ; heaven also was [its] canopy ; the two draft-oxen were white (cukra), when Surya went to her husband.
11. Haltered with verse (ic) and chant (sdman), thy two oxen went peaceful (? samand) ; ears were thy (two) wheels ; in the sky the wandering track.
12. Clean were the (two) wheels of thee as thou wentest ; out-breath-ing (vyana) was the instered axle ; a cart made of mind did Surya ascend when going forth to her husband.
13. The bridal (vahatu) of Surya, which Savitar sent off (ava-srj), has gone forth ; in the Maghas are slain the kine ; in the Phalgunis is the wedding.
14. When, O Acvins, ye went asking, with your three-wheeled [chariot], to Surya's bridal, where was one wheel of yours? Where stood ye for pointing out?
15. When ye went, O lords of beauty, unto the wooing of Surya, all the gods assented to that [deed] of yours ; Pushan as son chose a father.
16. The two wheels of thee, O Surya, the priests (hvahman) know sea-sonably ; further, the one wheel that is in secret - that, verily, the enlightened (addhati) know.

17. We make offering to Aryaman of good connections, husband-finder ; like a gourd from its bond, from here I release, not from yonder.

18. I release [her] from here, not from yonder ; I make her well-bound yonder, that she, O gracious Indra, may be rich in sons, well-portioned.

19. I release thee from Varuna's fetter, with which the very propitious Savitar bound thee ; in the lair (yoni) of righteousness, in the wooer (-sambhala).

20. Let Bhaga lead thee hence, grasping thy hand ; let the Acvins carry thee forth by a chariot ; go to the houses, that mayest be housewife ; thou, having control, shalt speak unto the councol.

21. Let what is dear succeed (sam-rdh) here for thy progeny ; watch thou over this house in order to housewife-ship ; mingle thy self (tanu) with this husband ; then shalt thou in advanced age speak to the council.

22. Be ye (two) just here ; be not separated ; attain your whole life-time, sporting with sons [and] grandsons, rejoicing, well-homed.

23. These two move on one after the other by magic ; two sporting young ones go about the ocean ; the one looks abroad upon all beings ; thou, the other, disposing the seasons art born new.

24. Ever new art thou, being born ; sign of the days, thou goes to the apex of the dawns ; thou disposest to the gods their share as thou comest ; thou extendest, O moon, a long life-time.

25. Give thou away the camulya; share out goods to the priests (brahman) ; it, becoming a walking (padvant) witchcraft. enters the husband [as] a wife.

26. It becomes blue-red ; [as] witchcraft, infection, it is driven away (?) ; her relations (jnati) thrive ; her husband is bound in bonds.

27. Unlovely becomes [his] body, glistening in that evil way, when the husband wraps his own member with the bride's garment.

28. Carving on, carving open, also cutting over apart ; see the forms of Surya ; them also the priest (brahman) cleans (cumbh).

29. Harsh is that, sharp, barbed, poisoned ; that is not to be eaten; what priest (brahman) knows Surya, he indeed deserves the bride's [garment].

30. That priest verily takes this garment, pleasant, well-omened, who goes over the expiation, by whom the wife takes no harm.

31. Do ye (two) bring together a successful (samrddha) potion, speaking right in right-speakings ; O Brahmanaspati, make the husband shine (ruc) for her ; let the wooer (sambhala) speak this speech agreeably (caru).

32. May ye be just here ; may ye not go away ; may ye, O kine, increase this man with progeny ; going un beauty, ruddy, with soma-splendor - may all the gods turn (kr) your mind hither.

33. May ye, O kine, enter this man together with progeny ; this man minisheth (mi) not the share of the gods ; for this man shall Pushan, and all the Maruts, for this man shall Dhatar, Savitar quicken (su) you.

34. Free from thorns, straight, let the roads be by which [our] comreds go a-wooing for us ; together with Bhaga, together with Aryaman - let Dhatar unite [us] with splendor.

35. Both what splendor is placed in dice, and what in strong drink - what splendor, O Acvins, is in kine, with that splendor favor (av) ye this woman.

36. With what [splendor] the backsides of the courtezan (mahanagni), O Acvins, or with what the strong drink, with what the dice were flooded (abhi-sic), with that splendor favor ye this woman.

37. He who shines (di) without fuel within the waters, whom the devout (vipra) praise at the sacrifices (adhvara) - O child of the waters, mayest thou give waters rich in honey, with which Indra increased, full of heroism.

38. Now do I remove (apa-uh) the glistening seizer (grabha), body-spoiling ; what sheen is excellent, that I draw up (ud-ac).

39. Let the Brahmans take for her [water] for bathing ; let them draw up (?) waters that slay not a hero ; let her go about the fire of Aryaman, O Pushan ; father-in-law and brother-in-law are looking on (prati-iks).

40. Weal be to thee gold, and weal be waters ; weal be the post (methi), weal the perforation (tardman) of the yoke ; weal be for thee the waters having a hundred cleaners (-pavitra) ; for weal, too, mingle thy-self with thy husband.

41. In the hole of the chariot, in the hole of the cart, in the hole of the yoke, O thou of a hundred activities, having thrice purified Apala, O Indra, thou didst make her sun-skinned.

42. Hoping for well-willing, offspring, good-fortune, wealth, becoming obedient (anuvrata) to thy husband, gird thyself in order to immortality.

43. As the [mighty (? Vrsa)] river (sindhu) won (? su) the supremacy of the streams (nadi), so be thou supreme (samrajni), having gone away to thy husband's home.

44. Be thou supreme among father-in-law, supreme also among brothers-in-law ; be thou supreme over sister-in-law, supreme also over mother-in-law.

45. They (f.) who spun, wove, and who stretched [the verb], what divine ones (f.) gave the ends about, let them wrap thee in order to old age ; [as] one long-lived put about thee this garment.

46. They bewail the living one (m.) ; they lead away the sacrifice (adhvara) ; the men sent their thoughts after [root dhi□anu] a long reach (prasiti) ; what is lovely (vama) for the Fathers who came together here ; joy to the husbands for embracing the wife.

47. I maintain for thee, in order to progeny, a pleasant, firm (dhruva) stone in the lap of the divine earth ; stand thou on that, one to be exulted after, of excellent glory ; let Savitar make for thee a long life-time.

48. Wherewith Agni grasped the right hand of this earth, therewith grasp I thy hand ; do not stagger in company with me, with both progeny and riches.

49. Let god Savitar grasp thy hand ; let king Soma make thee to have good offspring ; let Agni, Jatavedas, make the spouse well-portioned, long-lived, for her husband.

50. I grasp thy hand in order to good-fortune, that with me as husband thou mayest be long-lived ; Bhaga, Aryaman, Savitar, Purandhi [puramdhi] - the gods have given thee to me in order to housewifeship.

51. Bhaga hath grasped thy hand ; Savitar hath grasped thy hand ; thou art [my] spouse by ordinance (dharman), I thy house-lord.

52. Be this woman mine, bringing prosperity (posya) ; Brihaspati hath given thee to me ; in company with me [as husband] do thou live, rich in offspring, a hundred autumns.

53. Tvashtar disposed (vi-dha) the garment for beauty, by direction of Brihaspati, of the poets ; therewith let Savitar and Bhaga envelop this woman, like Surya, with progeny.

54. Let Indra-and-Agni, heaven-and-earth, Mataricvan, Mitra-and-Varuna, Bhaga, both Acvins, Brihaspati, the Maruts, the Brahman, Soma, increase this woman with progeny.

55. Brihaspati first prepared (klp) the hairs on the head of Surya ; eith this, O Acvins, do we thoroughly adorn (cubh) this woman for her husband.

56. This [is] that form in which the young woman (yosa) dressed herself ; I desire to know with [my] mind the wife (jaya) moving about ; I will go after her with nine-fold (? Navagva) comrades: who, knowing, unloosened (vi-crt) these fetters?

57. I loosen (vi-sa) in me the form of her ; he verily shall know, seeing the nest of mind ; I eat not stonely ; I was freed (ud-muc) by mind, myself untying (crath) the fetters of Varuna.

58. I release thee from Varuna's fetter, with which the very propious Savitar bound thee ; wide space (loka), an easy road here, do I make for thee, O bride (vadhu), with thy husband.

59. Raise ye [your weapons] ; may ye smite away the demon ; set this woman in what is well done ; inspired Dhatar found for her a husband ; let king Bhaga go in front, foreknowing.

60. Bhaga fashioned the four feet; Bhaga fashioned the four frame pieces (? Usyala); Tvashtaar adorned (pic) the straps (? vardhna) along in the middle; let her be to us of excellent omen.

61. The well-flowered (sukincuka), all-formed bridal-car (vahatu), golden colored, well-rolling, well-wheeked, do thou mount, O Surya, to the world of the immortal; make thou a bridal-car pleasant to husbands.

62. Her, not brother-slaying, O Varuna; not cattle-slaying, O Brihaspati; not husband-slaying, possessing sons, O Indra - bring [her] for us, O Savitar.

63. Injure ye not the maiden (kumari), ye (two) pillars, on the god-made road; the door of the divine house we make pleasant, a road for the bride.

64. Let the Brahman be yoked after, the Brahman before, the Brahman at the end, in the middle, the Brahman everywhere; going forward to an impenetrable stronghold of the gods, do thou (f.), propitious, pleasant, bear rule in thy husband's world.

Marriage ceremonies (continued)

1. For thee in the beginning they carried about Surya, together with the bridal-car ; mayest thou, O Agni, give to us husbands the wife, together with progeny.
2. Agni hath given back the spouse, together with life-time, he who is the husband of her live a hundred autumns.
3. Soma's wife first; the Gandharva thy next husband; Agni thy third husband; thy fourth, one of human birth.
4. Soma gave to the Gandharva ; the Gandharva gave to Agni; both wealth and sons hath Agni given to me, likewise this woman.
5. Your favor hath come, O ye (two) of abundant good things (? Vajinivasu); [our] desires have rested in [your] hearts, O Acvins ; ye have been twin keepers, O lords of beauty ; may we, being dear, attain favorers (aryaman) of our homes (? Durya).
6. Do thou (f.), rejoicing with propitious mind, assign wealth having all heroes, to be extolled ; an easy crossing (tirtha), well provided with drink, O lords (du.) of beauty ; do ye smite away the pillar standing in the road, [namely] disfavor.
7. What herbs [there are], what streams, what fields, what forests — let these, O bride, defend from the demon thee, possessing progeny, for thy husband.
8. We have mounted this road, easy, bringing welfare, on which a hero takes no harm, [but] finds others' goods.
9. Pray hear ye now of me, O men, by what blessing (acts) the two spouses attain what is agreeable (vama): what Gandharva [there are] and heavenly Apsarases, who stand upon these forest trees Uanaspatyd). Let them be pleasant unto this bride; let them not injure the bridal-car as it is driven.
10. what ydksmas go to the bride"s brilliant (candrd) car a mong the people let the worshipful goods conduct those back whence they came.
11. Let not the waylayers who pursu (them) find the two spouses;let them go over what is difficult by an easy (road) ; let the iggards run away.
12. I course the bridal-car to be viewed by the house with worship with a friendly, not terrible eye; what of all forms is fastend on about, let Savitar make that pleas ant for the husbands,

13. proposion hath this woman come to the home ; Dhatar appointed this world (Shere) to her ; her let Aryaman, Bhaga both Acvins prajapati, increase with progeny.
14. (As) a soulful cultivated field hath this woman come ; in her here, o man,scutter ye seed,she shall give birth to progeny for you from her belly bearing the exuded sperm of the male (rsabhd).
15. stand firm ; viraj art thou ; as it were, Vishnu here O Sarasvati ; O Sinivali, let her have progeny ; may she be in the favor of Bhaga.
16. Let your ware smite up the pegs ; O waters,release the yoke-ropse ; let not the inviolable (kine), not evil-doing free from guilt,come upon what is impropitous.
17. With an aye not terrible not husband-saying pleasant,helpful very propitious of easy control for the house, hero bearing loving brothes-in law (?),With favoring-may we thrive together with thee.
18. Not brother-in law slaying not husband-slaying be thou here propitious to the cattle,of easy control vary splendig having progeny hero-bearing loveing brothers-in law (?), pleasant, do thou worship this householder's fire.
19. Stand up from hare; desiring what hast thou (f.) come hither? I thine overcomer O Ida, out of own house; thou that hast come hither O perdition seeking the empty-stand up ; Oniggard ;fly forth ; rest not here.
20. When this bride hath worshiped the huseholder's the former fire, then, O woman, do thou pay homage to Sarasvati and to the Fathers.
21. Take this protection, defense, to spread under this woman ; O Sinivali, let her have progeny; may she be in the favor of Bhaga.
22. What rushes ye cast down, and hide ye spread under, that let the girl of good progeny mount, who finds a husband.
23. Spread under the rushes upon the red hide; sitting down upon it, of good progeny, let her worship this fire.
24. Mount the hide ; sit by the fire; this god slays all the demons ; here give birth to progeny for this husband ; may this son of thine be of good primogeniture.

25. Let there come forth from the lap of this mother animals of yarious forms, being born; as one of excellent omen, sit thou by this fire; with thy husband, be thou serviceable to the gods here.

26. Of excellent omen, extender of the houses, very propitious to thy husband, wealful to thy father-in-law, pleasant to thy mother-in-law, do thou enter these houses.

27. Be thou pleasant to father-in-law, pleasant to husband, to houses, pleasant to all this clan; pleasant unto their prosperity be thou.

28. Of excellent omen is this bride ; come together, see her; having given unto her good-fortune, go asunder and away with ill-fortunes.

29. What evil-heated young woman, and likewise what old ones, here—do ye all now give splendor to her ; then go asunder and away home.

30. The gold-cushioned vehicle, bearing all forms, did Surya, Savitar's daughter, mount, in order to great good-fortune.

31. Mount the couch with favoring mind; here give birth to progeny for this husband ; like Indrani, waking with good awakening, mayest thou watch to meet dawns tipped with light.

32. The gods in the beginning lay with their spouses ; they embraced bodies with bodies; like Surya, O woman, all-formed, with greatness, having progeny, unite here with thy husband.

33. Stand up from here, O Vicvavasu; with homage do we praise thee ; seek thou a sister sitting among the Fathers, inserted ; that is thy portion by right of birth ; know thou that.

34. The Apsarases revel a joint reveling, between the oblation-holder and the sun; they are thy birthplace ; go away to them ; homage I pay thee with the Gandharva-season.

35. Homage to the Gandharva's mind, and homage to his terrible eye we pay; O Vicvavasu, homage to thee with worship ; go away unto thy wives, the Apsarases.

36. With wealth may we be well-willing ; we have made the Gandharva go up from here; that god hath gone to the highest station; we have gone where they lengthen out [their] life-time.

37. Unite, O ye parents, the things that are seasonable ; ye shall be mother and father of seed ; as a male a female, do thou mount her; make ye progeny ; here rnjoy wealth.

38. Send, O Pushan, her, most propitious, in whom men scatter seed ; who, eager, shall part our thighs; in whom we, eager, may insert the member.

39. Mount thou the thigh ; apply the hand; embrace thy wife with well-willing mind ; make ye progeny here, enjoying ; let Savitar make for you a long life-time.

40. Let Prajapati generate progeny for you ; let Aryman unite [you] with days-and-night ; not ill-omened, enter thou this world of thy husband ; be weal to our bipeds, weal to [our] quadrupeds.

41. This bridal garment and bride's dress, given by the gods together with Manu, whoso gives to a knowing priest, he verily slays the demons of the couch.

42. What priest's portion they give to me the bride-seeker, the bridal garment and bride's dress, do ye O Brihaspati and Indra, assenting, together give it to the priest.

43. Awaking out of a pleasant lair, mightily enjoying your-salves, merry, having good kine, good sons, good houses, may ye, living, pass the outshining dawns.

44. Clothing myself anew, fragrant, well-dressed, I have risen alive unto the outshining dawns; as a bird from the egg, I have been released out of all sin.

45. Beautiful [are] heavan-and-earth, pleasant near by, of great courses; seven divine waters have flowed ; let them free us from distress.

46. Unto Surya, unto the gods, unto Mitra and Varuna, unto them who are forethoughtful of that which exists, have I paid this homage.

47. He who, without a clamp, before the piercing of the neck-ropes, combines a combination-he the bountiful, the one of much good—removes again what is spoiled.

48. Away from us let the darkness shine, that is deep blue, brown, also red ; she who is consuming, spotted, her I fasten on this pillar.

49. How many witchcrafrs in the outer garment, how many fetters of king Varuna, what failures, what non-successes—them I cause to sit upon this pillar.

50. What is my dearest self, that of me is afraid of the garment ; of it do thou, O forest-lord, make first for thyself an inner wrap; let us not suffer harm.

51. What ends [there are], how many edges, what webs, and what lines ; what garment woven by the spouses—may that touch us pleasantly.

52. Eager, these young girls, going to a husband from the father's world, have let go the consecration : hail !

53. Her, let go by Brihaspati, all the gods maintained ; what splendor is entered into the kine, with that do we unite this woman.

54. Her, let go etc. etc.; what brilliancy is entered etc. etc.

55. Her, let go etc. etc.; what fortune is entered etc. etc.

56. Her, let go etc. etc.; what glory is entered etc. etc.

57. Her, let go etc. etc.; what milk is entered etc. etc.

58. Her, let go etc. etc.; what sap is entered etc. etc.

59. If these hairy people have danced together in thy house, doing evil with wailing—from that sin let Agni and Savitar release thee.

60. If this daughter of thine has wailed with loosened hair in thy house, doing evil with wailing—from that sin etc. etc.

61. If sisters, if young women, have danced together in thy house, doing evil with wailing—from that sin etc. etc.

62. If in thy progeny, in thy cattle, or in thy houses is settled any evil done by the evil-doers—from that sin etc. etc.

63. This woman, scattering shriveled grains appeals: be my husband long-lived ; may he live a hundred autumns.

64. Here, O Indra, do thou push together these two spouses like two cakravakas; let them, with [their] progeny, well-homed, live out all their life-time.

65. What is done on the chair, on the cushion, or what on the covering ; what witchcraft they have made at the wedding—that do we deposit in the bath.

66. What ill deed, what pollution at the wedding, and what on the bridal car—that difficulty do we wipe off on the dress of the wooer.

67. Having settled the defilement on the wooer, the difficulty on the dress, we have become worshipful, cleansed; may he extend our life-times.

68. The artificial hundred-toothed comb (?) that is here shall scratch away the defilement of the hair of her, away that of her head.

69. Away from every limb of her do we deposit the yaksma; let that not attain the earth nor the gods; let it not attain the heaven, the wide atmosphere; let that defilement not attain the waters, O Agni; let it not attain Yama and all the Fathers.

70. I gird thee with the milk of the earth ; I gird thee with the milk of the herbs ; I gird thee with progeny, with riches; do thou, being girded, win this strength.

71. He am I, she thou ; chant am I, verse thou ; heaven I, earth thou; let us come together here; let us generate progeny.

72. The unmarried if us seek a wife, the liberal seek a son; may we, with uninjured life-breath, be companions, in order to what is great, to winning of strength.

73. What bride-beholding Fathers have come to this bridal-car, let them bestow on this bride, with her husband, protection accompanied with progeny.

74. She who hath come hither before, girdling herself (?), having given to this woman here progeny and property—her let them carry along the road of what is not gone; this one, a viraj, having progeny, hath conquered.

75. Continue thou awake, waking with good awakening, unto length of life of a hundred autumns; go to the houses that thou mayest be house-mistress; let Savitar make for thee a long life-time.

References from Atharvaveda on Genetics

Funeral Verses

1. Unto a friend would I turn with friendship ; having gone through much ocean, may the pious one take a grandson of [his] father, considering further onward upon the earth.

2. Thy friend wants not that friendship of thine, that she of like sign should become of diverse form; the sons of the great Asura, heroes, sustainers of the sky, look widely about.

3. Truly those immortals want that—posterity of the one mortal; may thy mind be set in our mind ; mayest thou enter [as] husband a wife's body.

4. What we did not do formerly, why [do that] now ? speaking righteousness, should we prate unrighteousness ? The Gandharva in the waters and the watery woman-that is our union, that our [du.] highest relation.

5. Verily, the generator made us in the womb man and spouse—god Tvashtar, Savitar of all forms; none overthrow his ordinances ; earth knows us [two] as such, also heaven.
6. Who yokes to the pole today the kine of righteousness, the diligent, the bright, the slow to wrath, that have arrows in the mouth that shoot at the heart, amiable ones ? whoso shall prosper their burden, he shall live.
7. Who knows of that first day ? Who saw it ? Who shall proclaim it here ? Great is the ordinance dhaman) of Mitra, of Varuna ; why, O lustful one, wilt thou speak to men with deceit (Vici)
8. Desire of Yama hath come unto me Yami, in order to lying together in the same lair (yoni) ; I would fain yield (ric) my body, as wife to husband ; may we whirl off, like two chariot wheels.
9. They stand not, they wink not, those spies of the gods who go about here ; with another than me, O lustful one, go quickly ; with him whirl off like two chariot wheels.
10. By nights, by days one may pay reverence (dacasy) to him ; the sun's eye may open (? Un mimiyat) for a moment ; with heaven, with earth paired, of near connection ; - Yami must bear the unbrotherly (djami) [conduct] of Yama.
11. Verily there shall come those later ages (Yuga) in which next of kin (jami) shall do what is unkindly (djami]. Put thine arm underneath a hero (vrsabha) ; seek, O fortunate one, another husband than me.
12. What should brother be when there is no protector ? or what sister, when destruction impends (ni-gam) ? Impelled by desire, I prate thus much ; mingle thou thy body with my body.
13. I am not thy protector here, O Yami ; I may not mingle my body with thy body ; with another than me do thou prepare enjoyments ; thy brother wants not that, O fortunate one.
14. Verily, I may not mingle my body with thy body ; they call him wicked (papa) who should approach his sister. That is not consonant (?asamydt) with my mind [and] heart, that I, a brother, should lie in a sister's bed (cayana).
15. A weakling (? Bata), alas, art thou, O Yama ; we have not found mind and heart thine ; verily, another woman shall embrace thee, as a girth a harnessed [horse], as twining plant (libuja) a tree.

16. Another man, truly, O Yami, another man shall embrace thee, as a twining plant a tree ; either do thou seek his mind or he thine ; then make for thyself very excellent concord (samvid)
17. Three meters the poets extended (? vi-yat) - the many-formed one, the admirable, the all-beholding ; waters, winds, herbs - these are set (drpita) in one being (bhuvana).
18. The bull yieldeth (duh) milks for the bull with the milking of the sky (div), he the unharmable son (? Yahva) or Aditi ; everything knoweth he, like Varuna, by thought (dhi) ; he, sharing the sacrifice (yajniya), sacrificeth to the seasons that share the sacrifice.
19. Prateth the Gandharvi and watery woman ; in the noise of the noisy one (nada) let [her] protect our mind ; let Aditi set us in the midst of what is desired (?ista) ; our oldest brother shall first speak out.
20. She now, the excellent, rich in food, full of glory - the dawn hath shone for man (manu), full of light (svar) ; since they have generated for the council [as] hotr. Agni, the eager one, after the will (kratu) of the eager ones.
21. Then that mighty (vibhu) conspicuous drop did the bird, the lively falcon, bring at the sacrifice ; if the Aryan tribes (vic) choose the wondrous one, Agni, [as] hotr, then prayer (dhi) was born.
22. Ever art thou pleasant (ranva) as pastures to him that tnuoys (pus) them, being, O Agni, well sacrificed to with the offerings of man (manus) ; or when, active, praiseworthy, having won the strength (vdja) of the inspired one (vipra), thou approachest with very many.
23. Send thou up the (two) fathers, [as] a lover, unto enjoyment (bhaga). The welcome one (haryata) desires to sacrifice he sends from the heart ; the bearer (vahni) speaks out; the merry one (?makha) does a good work ; the Asura shows might (tavisy) ; he trembles with purpose (?mati).
24. Whatever mortal hath seen thy favor, O Agni, son of power, he is nenowned exceedingly ; acquiring (dha) food (is), borne by horses, he, lightful, vigorous, passes (?a-bhus) the days (div.)
25. Hear us, O Agni, in thy seat, thy station ; harness the speedy chariot of the immortal (amrta) ; bring to us the two firmaments

(rodasi), parents of the gods ; be thou of the gods never (makis) away ; mayest thou be there.

26. That, O Agni, this meeting may take place (bhu), divine, amont the gods, worshipful, thou reverend one, and that thou mayest share out treasures, O self-ruling one, do thou enjoy here our portion filled with good things.

27. Agni hath looked after the apex of the dawns, after the days, [he] first, Jatavedas ; a sun, after the dawns, after the rays ; after heaven-and-earth he entered.

28. Agni hath looked forth to meet the apex of the dawns, to meet the days [he] first, Jatavedas, and to meet the rays of the sun in many places ; to meet heaven-and-earth he stretched out.

29. Heaven and earth, first by right, truth-speaking, are within hearing, when the god, making mortals to sacrifice, sits a hotr, going to meet his own being (asu).

30. A god, encompassing the gods with right, carry thou first our offering, understanding [it] ; smoke-bannered by the fuel, light-beaming, a pleasant, constant hotr, skilled sacrificer with speech.

31. I praise (arc) your (du.) work unto increase, ye ghree-surfaced ones ; O heaven-and-earth, hear me, ye two firmaments (rodasi); when days, O gods, went to the other life (asuniti). let the two parents (pitara) sharpen us here with honey.

32. It the god's immortality (amrta) is easy to appropriate for the cow, thence those who are born maintain themselves on the broad [earth]; all the gods go after that sacrifical formula of thine, when the hind yields (duh) the ghree, heavenly liquor (vdr).

33. Why forsooth hath the king seized (gran) us ? what have we done in transgression of (ati) his ordinance (vrata) ? who discerns [it] ? for even Mitra, swerving the gods, like a song of praise (cloak), is the might also of them that go.

34. Hard to reverence (? Durmantu) here is the name of the immortal, that she of like sign should become of diverse form ; whoso shall reverence Yama with proper reverence (? Sumantu), him, O Agni, exalted one, do thou protect, unremitting.

35. In whom the gods revel at the council, maintain themselves in Vivasvant's seat - they placed light in the sun, rays in the moon : the wo, unfailing, wait upon (pari-car) the brightness (dyotani).

36. In what secret (apicya) devotion (manman) the gods go about (sam-car) - we know it not ; may Mitra, may Aditi, may god Savitar declare us here guiltless to Varuna.

37. O companions, we would supplicate (a-cas) worship (Brahman) for Indra, possessor of the thunderbolt, to praise, indeed, the most manly, the daring.

38. For thou art famed for might (cavas), for Vritra-slaying, A Vritra-slayer ; thou out-bestowest the bounteous with thy bounties, O hero.

39. Thou goest over the earth as stega over the gound ; let winds blow here on the great earth (bhumi) for us ; Mitra for us there (atra), Varuna, being joined, hath let loose hear (coka), as fire does in the forest.

40. Praise thou the famed sitter on the hollow of men (jana), the terrible king, formidable assailant (? Upahatnu) ; being praised, O Rudra, be gracious to the singer ; let thine army (? senya) lay low (ni-vap) another than us.

41. On Sarasvati do the pious call ; on Sarasvati, while the sacrifice is being extended ; on Sarasvati do the well-doers call ; may Sarasvati give what is desirable to the worshiper (dacvdns).

42. On Sarasvati do the Fathers call, arriving at the sacrifice on the south ; sitting on this barhis do ye revel ; assign thou to us food (isas) free from disease.

43. O Sarasvati, that wentest in company (saratham) with the songs (uktha), with the svadhas, O goddess, reveling with the Fathers, assign thou to the sacrificer here a portion of refreshment (id) of thousandfold value, abundance of wealth.

44. Let the lower, let the higher, let the midmost Fathers the somadrinking (?somya), go up ; they who went to life (asu), unharmed (avrka), right-knowing - let those Fathers aid us at our calls.

45. I have won hither (a-vid) the beneficient Fathers, both the grandson and the wide-stridling of Vishu ; they who, sitting on the barhis, partake of the pressed drink with svadha - they come especially hither.

46. Be this homage today to the Fathers, who went first, who went after, who are seated in the space (rajas) of earth, or who are now in regions (dic) having good abodes (suvrjana).

47. Matali with the Kavyas, Yama with the Angirases, Brihaspati increasing with the rkvans ('praisers') ; both they whom the gods increased and who [increased] the gods - let those Father's aid us at out calls.

48. Sweet verily is this [soma], and full of honey is this ; strong (tivra) verily is this, and full of sap is this ; and no one soever overpowers in conflicts (ahava) Indra, having not drunk of it.

49. Him that went away to the advances called great, spying out the road for many, Vivasvant's son, gatherer of people, king Yama, honor (sapary) ye with oblation.

50. Yama first found for us a track gati) ; that is not a pasture to be borne away ; where our former Fathers went forth, there (end) [go] those born [of them], along their own roads.

51. Ye barhis-seated Father's hitherward with aid ! these offerings have we made for you ; enjoy [them] ! do ye come with most wealful aid ; then assign to us weal [and] profit, free fom evil.

52. Bending the knee, sitting down on the right, let all assent to (abhi-gr) this libation of ours ; injure us not, O Fathers, by reason of any offense (agas) which we may do to you through humanity.

53. Tvashtar makes a wedding-car for his daughter ; by reason of this, all this creation comes together ; the mother of Yama, wife of great Vivasvant, being drawn about, disappeared.

54. Go thou forth, go forth by roads that go to the stronghold (puryana), as (yena) thy Fathers of old went forth ; both kings, reveling with svadha, shalt thou see, Yama and god Varuna.

55. Go ye away, go asunder, and creep apart from here ; for this man the Fathers have made this world ; adorned with days, with waters, with rays (aktu), a rest (avasana) Yama gives to him.

56. Eager (ucant) would we light thee, eager would we kindle ; do thou, eager, bring the eager Fathers to eat the oblation.

57. Lightful (dyumant) would we light thee, lightful would we kindle ; do thou, lightful, bring the lightful Fathers to eat the oblation.

58. The Angirases, our naivagva Fathers, the Atharvans, the Bhrigus, soma-drinkers (somya) - may we be in the favour of those worshipful ones, likewise in their excellent well-willing.

59. Come thou hither with the worshipful Angirases ; revel here, O Yama, with the Vairupas - I call Vivasvant, who is thy father - sitting down upon this barhis.

60. Ascend thou, O Yama, this cushion (prastara), in concord with the Angiras Fathers; let the sacred utterances (mantra) made in praise by the poets bring thee ; then (end), O king, revel thou in the oblation.

61. These ascended up from here ; they ascended the backs of the sky (div) ; the Angirases have gone forth to heaven (div), like bhurjis, by the road.

Funeral Verses : Genetics

1. For Yama to soma purifies itself ; for Yama is made the oblation; to Yama goes the sacrifice, messengered by Agni, made satisfactory.
2. Offer ye to Yama what is most honeyed, and stand forth ; this homage to the former-borne, the former, the path-making seers.
3. Unto Yama the king offer ye an oblation, milk rich in ghee ; he furnishes (a-yam) to us among the living a long life-time, for living on.
4. Do not, O Agni, burn him up ; do not be hot upon (abhi-cuc) him; do not warp (ksip) his skin, nor his body ; when thou shalt make him done, O Jatavedas, then send him forward unto the Fathers.
5. When thou shalt make done, O Jatavedas, then commit him to the Fathers ; when he shall go to that other life (asuniti), then shall he become a controller (?vacant) of the gods.
6. With the trikadrukas it purifies itself ; six wide ones, verily one great one ; tristubh, gayatri, the meters ; all those [are] set in Yama.
7. Go thou to the sun with thine eye, to the wind with thy soul (atman) ; go both to heaven and to earth with [their] due shares (?dharman) ; or go to the waters, if there it is acceptable (hita) to thee ; in the herbs stand firm with thy bodies.
8. The goat is the share of the heat (tapas) ; heat thou that ; that let thine ardor (cocis) heat, that thy flame (arcis) ; what propitious bodies (tanu) are thine, O jatavesas, with them carry him to the world of the well-doing.

9. What ardors (coci), swiftnesses (ranhi) are thine, O Jatavedas, with which thou fillest the sky, the atmosphere, let them collect (sam-r) after the goat as he goes ; then with other most propitious ones make him propitious.

10. Release again, O Agni, to the Fathers him who goes (car) offered to thee, with Svadha ; clothing himself in life (dyus), let him go unto [his] posterity (?cesas) ; let him be united with a body, very splendid.

11. Run thou past the two four-eyed, brindled dogs of Sarama, by a happy (sadhu) road; then go unto the beneficent Fathers, who revel in common revelry with Yama.

12. What two defending dogs thou hast, O Yama, four-eyed, sitting by the road, men-watching, with them, O king, do thou surround him ; assign to him well-being and freedom from disease.

13. Broad-nosed, feeding on lives (? asutrp), copper-colored, Yama's two messangeres to about after men (jana) ; let them give us back here today excellent life (asu), to see the sun.

14. Soma purifies itself for some ; some wait upon (upa-as) ghee ; for whom honey runs forward (?), unto them do thou go.

15. They who of old were won by right, born of right, increasers of right - to the seers rich in vervor (tapas-), born of fervor, O Yama, do thou go.

16. They who by fervor are unassailable, who by fervor have gone to heaven (svar), who made fervor their greatness, unto them to thou go.

17. They who fight in the contests (pradhana), who are self-sacrificing (tanuiyaj) heroes, or who give thousand-fold sacrifical gifts, unto them do thou go.

18. Poets (kavi) of a thousand lays (nitha), who guard the sun — to the seers rich in fervor, born of fervor, O Yama, do thou go.

19. Be pleasant to him, O earth, a thornless resting-place ; furnish him broad refuge.

20. In the unoppressive wide space (lokd) of earth be thou deposited ; what svadhas thou didst make when living, be they dripping with honey for thee.

21. I call thy mind hither with mind ; come unto these houses, enjoying [them] ; unite thyself with the Fathers, with Yama ; let pleasant, helpful (?cagma) winds blow thee unto [them].

22. Let the water-carrying, water-floating Maruts carry thee up, making [thee] cool by the goat, let them sprinkle [thee] with rain, splash !

23. I have called up life-time unto life-time, unto ability (Kratu), unto dexterity, unto life, let thy mind go to its own [pl.] ; then run unto the Fathers.

24. Let nothing whatever of thy mind, nor of thy life (asu.) nor of thy members, nor of thy sap, nor of thy body, be left here.

25. Let not the tree oppress thee, nor the great divine earth ; havind found a place (loka) among the Fathers, thrive (edh) thou among those whose king is Yama.

26. What limb of thine is put over at a distance, and what expiration [or] breath has gone forth upon the wind (?), let the associated (sanida) Fathers, assembling, make that enter thee again, bit (ghasa) from bit.

27. The living have excluded this man from their houses ; carry ye him out, forth from this village ; death was the kindly messenger of Yama ; he made his life - breaths (asu) go to the Fathers.

28. What barbarians (dasyu), having entered among the Fathers, having faces of acquaintances, to about, eating what is not sacrificed, who bear parapur [and] nipour — Agni shall blast (dham) them forth from this sacrifice.

29. Let there enter together (sam-vic) here our own Fathers, doing what is pleasant, lengthening [our] life-time ; may we be able to reach them with oblation, living long for numerous autumns.

30. What milch-cow I set down (ni-pr) for thee, and what rice-dish for thee in milk (ksira) — with that mayest thou be the supporter of the person (jana) who is there (atra) without a living

31. Pass forward [over a stream] rich in horses, which is very propitious, or, further on, an rksaka, more new ; he who slew thee, be he one to be killed ; let him not find any other portion.

32. Yama beyond, below Vivasvant — beyond that do I see nothing whatever ; into Yama has entered my sacrifice, ; Vivasvant stretched after the worlds (bhu).

33. They hid away the immortal one (f.) from mortals ; having made one of like color, they gave her to Vivasvant ; what that was carried also the two Acvins ; and Sarayu deserted two twins.

34. They that are buried, and they that are scattered (vap) away, they that are burned and they that are set up (uddhita) — all those Fathers, O Agni, bring thou to eat the oblation.

35. They who, burned with fire, [and] who, not burned with fire, revel on svadha in the midst of heaven — them thou knowest, if thine, O Jatavedas ; let them enjoy with svadha the sacrifice, the suvidhiti.

36. Burn (tap) thou propitiously (cam) ; do not burn overmuch ; O Agni, do not burn the body ; be thy vehemence (cusma) in the wookds ; on the earth be what is thy violence (haras).

37. I give this release to him who hath thus come and hath become mine here — thus replies the knowing Yama — let this one approach (upa-stha) my wealth here.

38. This measure do we measure, so that one may not measure further ; in a hundred autumns, not before.

39. This measure do we measure forth, so that etc. etc.

40. This measure do we measure off, so that etc. etc.

41. This measure do we measure apart, so that etc. etc.

42. This measure do we measure out, so that etc. etc.

43. This measure do we measure up, so that etc. etc.

44. This measure do we measure together, so that etc. etc.

45. I have measured the measure, I have gone to heaven (svdr) ; may I be long-lived so that etc. etc.

46. Breath, expiration, through-breahing (vyana), life-time, an eye to see the sun : by a road not beset with enemies (para) go thou to the Fathers whose king is Yama.

47. They that departed unmarried [but] assiduous, abandoning hatreds, having no progeny — they, going up to heaven (div), have found a place (loka), [they,] shining (?didhyana) upon the back of the firmament.

48. Watery is the lowest heaven (div), full of stars (?pilu) is called the midmost ; the third is called the fore-heaven (pradiv), in which the Fathers sit.

49. They that are our father's fathers, that are [his] grandfathers, that entered the wide atmosphere, they that dwell upon earth and heaven (div) — to those Fathers would we pay worship with homage.

50. This time, verily, not further (aparam), seest thou the sun in the heaven (div) ; as a mother her son with her hem (sic), do thou cover him, O earth.

51. This, time, verily ; not further ; in old age another further than this ; as a wife her husband with her garment, do thou cover him, O earth (bhumi)

52. I cover thee excellently with the garment of mother earth ; what is excellent among the living, that with me ; svdha amongh the Fathers, that with thee.

53. O Agni-and-Soma, makers of roads, ye have distributed (vi-dha) to the gods a pleasant treasure [and] world ; send ye unto [us] Pushan, who shall carry by goat-traveled roads him that goes thither.

54. Let Pushan, knowing, urge thee forth from here — he, the shepherd of creation (bhuvana) who loses no cattle ; may he commit thee to those Fathers, [and] Agni to the beneficent gods.

55. May life-time, having all life-time, protect thee about ; let Pushan protect thee in front on the forward road ; where sit the well-doers, whither they have gone, there let god Savitar set thee.

56. I yoke for thee these two conveyers [vdhni], to convey (vah) thee to the other life; with them to Yama's seat and to the assemblies go thou down (dva)

57. This garment hath now come first to thee ; remove (apauh) that one which thou didst wear here before ; knowing, do thou follow along with what is offered and bestowed, where it is given thee variously among them of various connection (?vibandhu).

58. Wrap about thee of kine a protection from the fire ; cover thyself up with grease and fatness, lest the bold one, exulting with violence (haras), shake thee strongly (dadrh) about, intending to consume thee.

59. Taking the staff from the hand of the deceased man (gatasu), together with hearing, splendor, strength — thou just there, here may we, rich is heroes, conquer all scorners [and] evil plotters.

60. Taking the bow from the hand of the dead man, together with authority (ksatra), splendor, strength — take thou hold upon much prosperous good ; come thou hitherward unto the world of the living.

Funeral Verses

1. This woman, choosing her husband's world, lies down (ni-pad) by thee that art departed, O mortal, continuing to keep [her] ancient duty (dharma) ; to her assign thou here progeny and property.
2. Go up, O woman, to the world of the living ; thou liest by (upa-ci) this one who is deceased ; come ! to him who grasps thy hand, thy second spouse (didhisu), thou hast now entered into the relation of wife to husband.
3. I saw the maiden being led, being led about, alive, for the dead; as she was enclosed with blind darkness, then I led her off-ward (apaci) from in front (praktas).
4. Foreknowing, O inviolable one, the world of the living, moving together [with him] upon the road of the gods — this is thy herdsman (gopati) ; enjoy him ; make him ascend to the heavenly (svargd) world.
5. Unto sky (div), unto reed, more helpful of streams ; O Agni, gall of the waters art thou.
6. Whom thou, O Agni, didst consume, him do thou extinguish again ; let there grow here the kydmbu, the candadurvd, the vyalkaca.
7. Here is one for thee, beyond is one for thee ; enter thou into union with the third light ; at entrance be thou fair (crdu) with [thy] body, loved of the gods in the highest station.
8. Rise thou, go forth, run forth ; make thee a home (okas) in the sea [as] station ; there do thou, in concord with the Fathers, revel with soma, with the svadhas.
9. Start (cyu) forward, collect (sam-bhr) thy body ; let not thy limbs (gatra) nor thy frame (carira) be left out ; enter together after thy mind that has entered ; wherever in the world thou enjoyest, thither go.
10. Let the soma-drinking (somya) Fathers anoint me with splendor, the gods with honey, with ghee ; making me pass further on unto sight, let them increase me, attaining old age, unto old age.

11. Let Agni anoint me completely with splendor ; let Vishnu anoint wisdom into my mouth ; let all the gods fix wealth upon me ; let pleasant waters purify me with purifiers.

12. Mitra-and-Varuna have enclosed (pari-dha) me ; let the sacrificial posts of Aditi increase me ; let Indra anoint splendor into my hands ; let Savitar make me one attaining old age.

13. Him who died first of mortals, who went forth first to that world, Vivasvant's son, assembler of people, king Yama honor ye with oblation.

14. Go away, ye Fathers, and come ; this sacrifice is all anointed with honey for you ; both give to us here excellent property, and assign to us wealth having all heroes.

15. Let Kanva, Kakshivant, Purumidha, Agastya, Cyavacva, Sobharti, Archananas, Vicvamitara, Jamadagni here, Atri Kacyapa, vamadeva, aid us.

16. O Vicvamitra, Jamadagni, Vasishtha, Bharadvaja, Gotama, Vamadeva — Atri hath taken (grabh) our cardis with obeisances; ye Fathers of good report, be gracious to us.

17. They overpass defilement, wiping off in the metal bowl, assuming further on newer life-time, filling themselves up with progeny and riches ; then may we be of good odor in the houses.

18. They anoint, they anoint out, they anoint together ; they lick the rite, they smear with honey ; the bull flying in the river, the victim do the gold-purifiers seize in them.

19. What of you is joyous, O Fathers, and delectable, there with be at hand, for ye are of own splendor ; do ye, rapid poets, listen, beneficent, invoked at the council.

20. Ye who are Atris, Angirases, Navagvas, having sacrificed, attached to giving, bestowers, and who are rich in sacrificial fees, well-doing - do ye revel, sitting on this barhis.

21. So then as our distant Fathers, the ancient ones, O Agni, sharpening the rite : they went to the bright, they shone, praising with song ; splitting the ground, they uncovered the ruddy ones.

22. Of good actions, well-shining, pious, heavenly ones, forging the generations as metal, brightening Agni, increasing Indra, they have made for us a wide conclave, rich in kine.

23. As herbs at food, the formidable one hath looked over the cattle, the births of the gods, near by ; mortals have lamented the urvacis, unto the increase of the pious, of the next man.

24. We have made for thee we have been very active; the illuminating dawns have shone upon rite ; all that is excellent which the gods favor; may we talk big at the council, having good heroes.

25. Let Indra with the Maruts protect me from the eastern quarter ; arm-moved the earth, as it were to the sky above ; to the worldmakers, the road-makers, do we sacrifice, whoever of you are here, sharing in the oblation of the gods.

26. Let Dhatar protevt me from perdition from the southern quarter; arm-moved etc. etc.

27. Let Aditi with the Adityas protect me from the western quarter; arm-moved etc. etc.

28. Let Soma with all the gods protect me from the northern quarter; arm-moved etc. etc.

29. Dhartar the maintainer shall maintain thee aloft, as Savitar the light to the sky above ; to the world-makers etc. etc.

30. In the eastern quarter, away from approach, do I set thee in svadha; arm-moved etc. etc.

31. In the southern quarter, away etc. etc.

32. In the western quarter, away etc. etc.

33. In the northern quarter, away etc. etc.

34. In the fixed quarter, away etc. etc.

35. In the upward quarter, away etc. etc.

36. Dhartar art thou; maintaining art thou; bull art thou.

37. Water-purifyingart thou;honey-purifying art thou; wind-purifying art thou.

38. Both from here and from yonder let them aid me. As ye went pressing on like two twins, godloving men bring you forward; sit ye, on thine own place, knowing.

39. Be ye comfortable for our soma.

40. Three steps the form ascended, it went after the four footed one with its course ; it matches the song with the syllable ; in the navel of right it purifies.

41. For the gods he chose death ; for his progeny did he not choose immortality ? Brihaspati seer extended the sacrifice; Yama left his dear self.

42. Thou, O Agni, Jatavedas, being praised, hast carried the offerings, having made them fragrant ; thou hast given to the Fathers; they have eaten after their wont ; eat thou, O god, the presented oblations.

43. Sitting in the lap of the ruddy ones, assign ye wealth to your mortal worshiper; of that good, O Fathers, present ye to your sons; do ye bestow refreshment here.

44. Ye fire-sweetened Fathers, come hither; sit on each seat, well-conducting ones; eat on the barhis the presented oblations, and assign to us wealth having all heroes.

45. Called unto our delectable Fathers, to dear deposits on the barhis; let them come ; let them listen here; let them bless, let them aid us.

46. They who, our father's fathers, who grandfathers, followed after the soma-drinking, best ones—with them let Yama, sharing his gift of oblations, he eager with them eager, eat at pleasure.

47. They who thirsted panting among the gous, knowers of offering, praise-fashioned, with songs—come, O Agni, with the thousand god-revering true poets, seers sitting at the gharma,

48. The true, oblation-eating, oblation-drinking, that in alliance with the gods, with strong Indra—come hither ward, O Agni, with the beneficent, exalted, ancient seers, sitting at the gharma.

49. Approach thou this mother earth, the wide-expanded earth, the very propitious; the earth soft as wool to him who has sacrificial gifts; let her protect thee on the forward road in front.

50. Swell thou up, O earth; do not press down; be to him easy of access, easy of approach ; as a mother her son with her skirt, do thou, O earth, cover him.

51. Let the earth kindly remain swelling up, for let a thousand props support it ; let these houses, dripping with ghee, pleasant, be forever a refuge for him there.

52. I brace up (ut-stabh) the earth from about thee ; setting down this clod (?loga), let me take no harm ; this pillar do the Fathers maintain for thee ; let Yama there make seats for thee.

53. This bowl, O Agni, do not wrap (vi-hvr) ; [it is] dear to the gods and the delectable [Fathers] ; this bowl here for the gods to drink from — in it let the immortal gods revel.

54. The bowl that Atharvan bore full to Indra the vigorous, in that he makes a draught of what is well done ; in that, soma (indu) ever purifies itself.

55. What of thee the black bird cakuna) thrust at, the ant, the serpent, or also the beast of prey (cvapada), let the all-eating [vicva-ad] Agni make that free from disease, and the soma that hath entered the Brahmans.

56. Rich in milk are the herbs ; rich in milk is my milk ; what is the milk of the milk of the waters, therewith let one beautify (cubh) me.

57. Let these women, not widows, well-spoused, touch themselves with ointment, with butter ; terless, without disease, with good treasures, let the wives ascend first to the place of union.

58. Unite thyself (sam-gam) with the Fathers, with Yama, with thy sacred and charitable works in the highest firmament ; abandoning what is reproachful, come again home ; — let him himself with a body, very splendid.

59. They that are our father's fathers, that are [his] grandfathers, that entered the wide atmosphere — for them may the autocratic (svaraj) second life today shape our bodies as he will.

60. Let the mist be weal for thee ; let the frost fall down [as] weal for thee ; O cool one, possessing cool ones ; O refreshing one, possessing refreshing ones ; mayest thou be with weal a she-from in the waters ; kindly pacify thou this fire.

61. Let Vivasvant make for us freedom from fear, he who is well-preserving, quick-giving (?-dann), well-giving ; let these heroes be many here ; let there be in me prosperity (pousta) rich in kine, rich in horses.

62. Let Vivasvant set us in immortality ; let death go away ; let what is immortal come to us ; let [him] defend these men until old age ; let not their life-breaths (asu) go to Yama.

63. He who maintains himself by his might, like [birds?] in the atmosphere, poet of the Fathers, favorer (?pramati) of prayers (mati) — him praise ye, allbefriended, with oblations ; may that Yama give (dha) us to live further on.

64. Ascend ye to the highest heaven ; O seers, be not atraid ; ye soma-drinkers, soma-drenchers, this oblation is made to you ; we have gone to the highest light.

65. Agni shines forth with great show (ketu) ; the bull roars loudly unto the two firmaments (rodasi) ; [even] from the end of heaven he hath attained unto me (?) ; in the lap of the waters the buffalo increased.

66. As, longing with the heart, they looked upon thee, flying up* [as] an eagle in the firmament (naka), golden-winged messenger of Varuna, busy (bhuranyu) bird (cakuna) in the lair of Yama.

67. O Indra, bring us ability (kratu), as a father to his sons ; help (ciks) us in this course (yaman), O much-invoked one ; may we, living, attain to light.

68. What vessels covered (api-dha) with cakes the gods maintained for thee, be they for thee rich in svadha, rich in honey, dripping with ghee.

69. What grains I scatter along for thee, mixed with sesame, rich in svadha, be they for thee abundant (vibhu) prevailing ; them let king Yama approve for thee.

70. Give back, O forest tree, him who is deposited here with thee, that in Yama's seat he may sit speaking counsels.

71. Take hold, O Jatavedas ; let thy seizure (haras) be with sharpness (tejas-) ; his body do thou consume ; then set him in the world of the well-doing.

72. What Fathers of thine went away earlier and what later, for them let there go a brook of ghee, hundred-streamed, overflowing.

73. Ascend thou this, gaining (ud-mrj) vigor (vdyas) ; thine own [people] shine here greatly ; go forth, unto [them], — be not left behind midway — unto the world of the Fathers that is first there.

Funeral Verses

1. Ascend to [your] generatrix, ye Jatavedases ; by [roads] that the Fathers travel I make you ascend together ; the offering-carrier, sent out, hath carried the offerings ; united (yukta). Set ye him who hath sacrificed in the world of the well-doing.

2. The gods, the seasons, arrange the sacrifice, the oblation, the sacrificial cake, the ladles sruc), the implements (-ayudha) of sacrifice; with them go thou by roads that the gods travel, by which they that have sacrificed go to the heavenly svarga) world.
3. Look thou happily (sadhu) along the road of righteousness, by which go the Angirases, well-doers; by those roads go thou to heaven (svarga), where the Adityas feed on honey ; spread thou out upon the third firmament.
4. Three eagle (suparna) upon the back of the firmament (naka), at the summit (?vistap) are set (crita) ; let the heavenly (svarga) worlds, filled (?) with amrta, yield (duk) food, refreshment to the sacrificer.
5. The sacrificial spoon (juhu) sustains the sky, the offering spoon (upabhrt) the atmosphere ; the ladle (dhruva) sustains [dhr] the earth, the support (pratistha) ; unto me (?) let the worlds, ghee-backed, heavenly (svarga), yield every desire for the sacrificer.
6. O ladle, ascend the all-nourishing earth ; stride, O offering spoon, unto the atmosphere ; O sacrifical spoon, go to the sky (div) in company with the sacrificer ; with the little spoon (sruva) [as] calf, milk thou all the teeming, unirritated quarters.
7. By fords they cross the advances (pravat) called the great ones, by what [road] the sacrifices-makers, the well-doers, go; there did they set a world for the sacrificer, when they arranged the quarters, the creatures (bhuta).
8. The track (ayana) of the Angirases is the eastern fire ; the Adityas' track is the householder's fire ; the track of the sacrifical gifts is the sourthern fire, do thou, with thy limbs, whole (sarva) , powerful (?cagma), go unto the greatness of Agni [as] disposed by Brahman.
9. Let the eastern fire burn (tap) thee happily (cam) in front ; let the householder's fire burn happily behind ; let the southern fire burn refuge, defense for thee; from the north, from the midst, from the atmosphere, from each quarter, O Agni, protect him round about from what is terrible.
10. Ye, O Agni, having become back-carrying (?prstivah) horses, shall with most healthful forms (tanu) carry him that has sacrificed unto the heavenly (svarga) world, where they revel in common revelry with the gods.

11. Burn (tap), O Agni, happily behind, happily in front ; burn him happily above, happily below ; being one, O jatavedas, triply disposed, set him collectedly (samyak) in the world of the well-doers.
12. Let the fires, kindled, take hold happily; let the Jatavedases, making done (crid) here him that is Prajapati's [and] sacrificial, not throw him down.
13. The sacrifices goes, extended, adapting itself (?klp), [taking] him who hath sacrified, unto the heavenly (svarga) world ; let the fires enjoy it, made a whole oblation ; let the Jatavedases, making done here him that is Prajapati's [and] sacrificial, not throw him down.
14. He that hath sacrified ascended the piled fire, about to fly up to heaven(div) from the back of the firemament (naka) ; for him, the well-doer, shines forth from the welking (nabhas), full of light, the heavenly road, traveled by the gods.
15. Agni thine invoker, Brihaspati thine officiating priest, be Indra on the right thy supervising priest (Brahman) ; this offered sacrifice, being completed (samsthita), goeth where is the ancient track of those offered.
16. Rich in cakes, rich in milk (ksira-) let the dish (caru) take seat here ; to the world-makers, the road-makers, do we sacrifice, whoever of you are here, sharing in the oblation of the gods.
17. Rich in cakes, rich in curds (dadhi-), let the dish etc. etc.
18. Rich in cakes, rich in drops (drapsa-), let the dish etc.etc.
19. Rich in cakes, rich in ghee, let the dish etc. etc.
20. Rich in cakes, rich in flesh (mansa-), let the dish etc. etc.
21. Rich in cakes, rich in food, let the dish etc. etc.
22. Rich in cakes, rich in honey, let the dish etc. etc.
23. Rich in cakes, rich in sap, let the dish etc. etc.
24. Rich in cakes, rich in water (apa-), let the dish etc. etc.
25. What vessels covered with cakes the gods maintained for thee, be they for thee rich in svadha, rich in honey, dripping with ghee.
26. What grains I scatter along for thee, mixed with sesame, rich in svadha, be they for thee uprising (udbhu), prevailing ; them let king, Yama approve for thee.

27. A more abundant inexhaustibleness.

28. The drop leaped (skand) toward the earth, the sky (div), toward both this lair (yoni) and the one that was of old ; of the drop that goes about toward the same lair do I make oblation, after seven invocations (hotra).

29. A hundred-streamed Vayu, a heaven-finding sun (?arka), wealth, do those men-beholders look upon ; whose bestow (pr) and present (prayama) always, they milk a sacrificial gift having seven mothers.

30. They milk a receptacle (koca), a jar with four orifices, ida [as] milch-cow rich in honey, in order to well-being ; reveling refreshment, Aditi among the people, injure thou not, O Agni, in the highest firmament (vyoman).

31. This garment god Savitar gives thee to wear (bhr) ; putting on that, which is tarpya, do thou go about in Yama's realm.

32. The grains became a milch-cow ; the seasame became her calf ; upon her, unexhausted, one lives in Yama's realm.

33. Be these, O so-and-so, thy milch-kine that yield what is desired ; variegated, white, of like from, of different form, with sesame as calf, let them wait upon (upa-stha) thee there.

34. Grains variegated, yellow, white, grains black, red, [be] thy muchkine here ; with sesame as calf, yielding (duh) him refreshment, be they ever unresisting.

35. In Vaicvanara I offer this oblation, a thousand-fold, hundred-streamed fountain (utsa) ; it supports (bhr) [our] father, grandfathers ; [our] great-grandfathers it supports, swelling.

36. A thousand-streamed, hundred-stramed fountain, unexhausted, expanded upon the back of the sea, yielding refreshment, unresisting, do the Fathers wait on at their will (?svadhabhis).

37. This funeral pile (?kasambu) [is] piled with piling ; come, ye [his] fellows, look down at it ; this mortal goeth to immortality ; make ye houses for him according to his kindred.

38. Be thou just here, winning riches, with thought here, with ability here ; be thou here, very heroic, vigor-bestowing, not smitten away.

39. These waters, rich in honey, satisfying (abhi-trp) son [and] grandson, yielding to the Fathers svadha [and] amrta — let the heavenly waters gratify both sides.

40. O waters, send forth (pra-hi) Agni unto the Fathers : this sacrifice of mine let the Fathers enjoy ; they who attach themselves unto a sitting refreshment, may they confirm to us wealth having all heroes.

41. They kindle the immortal one, oblation-carrying, ghee loving; he knoweth the deposited deposits, the Fathers that are gone away to the distance.

42. What stirabout for thee, what rice-dish, what flesh I offer (ni-par) to thee, be they rich in svadha, rich in honey, dripping with ghee.

43. What grains I scatter along for thee, mixed with sesame, rich in svadha, be they for thee abundant, prevailing ; them let king Yama approve for thee.

44. This [is] the former, the after down-track, by which thy former Fathers went away ; they who are the forerunners, the followers (? abhisac) of it, they carry thee to the well-doing.

45. On Sarasvati do the pious call ; on Sarasvati, while the sacrifice is being extended ; on Sarasvati do the well-doers call ; may Sarasvati give what is desirable to the worshiper.

46. On Sarasvati do the Fathers call, arriving at the sacrifice on the south ; sitting on this barhis, do ye revel ; assign thou to us food free from disease.

47. O Sarasvati, that wentest in company with the songs, with the svadha, O goddess, reveling with the Fathers, assign thou to the sacrificer here a portion of refreshment of thousand-fold value, abundance of wealth.

48. Thee, being earth, I make enter into earth ; may god Dhatar lengthen out our life-time ; let him that goeth very far away be a finder of good for you ; then may the dead (pl.) come to be (sam-bhu) among the Fathers.

49. Start ye (du.) forward hither, wipe off that which the portents (? Abhibha) have said there of you ; from that come ye, inciolable ones, to this which is better, being bestowers here on me, a giver to the Fathers.

50. This sacrificial gift hath come excellently to us, given by him, well-milking, vigor-bestowing ; old age, coming close to (? Upa-prc) them living in youth, shall lead these away together unto the Fathers.

51. This barhis I bring forward for the Fathers ; a living, higher one I strew for the gods ; that do thou ascend, O man, becoming sacrificial ; let the Fathers acknowledge thee who art departed.

52. Thou hast sat upon this barhis, thou hast become sacrificial ; let the Fathers acknowledge thee who art departed ; collect thy body according to its joints ; I arrange thy members with Brahman.

53. King leaf is the cover of the dishes ; the strength of refreshment, the power, vigor, hath come to us, dispensing (vi-dha) life-time to the living (pl.) in order to length of life for a hundred autumns.

54. The share of refreshment that generated this man ; —the stome attained (gam) the overlordship of the foods; —him praise ye, all befriended, with oblation ; may that Yama make (dha) us tho live further.

55. As the five clans (manava) scattered (vap) a dwelling (harmya) for Yama, so do I scatter a dwelling, that there may be many of me (?)

56. Wear (bhr) thou this gold, which thy father wore before ; of thy father, going to heaven (svarga), do thou wipe off the right hand.

57. Both those who are living and those who are dead ; those who are born and those who are worshipful — for them let there go a brook of ghee, honey-streamed, overflowing.

58. There purifies itself the conspicuous bull of the prayers, the sun of days, lengthener out of dawns, of the sky (div) ; the breath of the rivers hath made the jars to resound loudly ; entering Indra's hearth with skill.

59. Let thy sparkling (?tvesa) smoke cover, being in the sky, extended bright ; for thou, O purifier, shinest like the sun with luster, with beauty (krpa).

60. Soma (indu) verily goes forward to Indra's rendezvous ; the comrade does not violate (prami) the comrade's agreements ; thou rushest to join, as a male after females — soma, in the jar, by a road of a hundred tracks.

61. They have eaten ; they have revelled [surely] ; they have shaken off (ava) those that are dear ; having own brughtness svabhanu), they have praised : inspired, youngest, we implore.

62. Come ye, O Fathers, delectable, by profound roads that the Fathers travel, assigning to us lifetime and progeny ; and do ye attach yourselves to us with abundances of wealth.

63. Go away, O Fathers, delectable, by profound roads that go to the stronghold (puryana) ; then in a month, come ye again to our houses to eat the oblation, with good progeny, with good heroes.

64. What one limb of you Agni Jatavedas left when making you go to the Fathers world, that same for you I fill up again ; revel eye, O Fathers, in heaven svarga) with [all] your limbs.

65. Jatavedas has been the messenger sent forth, at evening, at close of day to be honored by men ; — thou hast given to the Fathers ; they have eaten after their wont ; eat thou, O god, the presented oblations.

66. Thou yonder, ho ! hither thy mind ! as sisters (jami) a kakutsala, do thou cover him, O earth.

67. Let the worlds where the Fathers sit adorn themselves (cumbh) ; I make thee to sit in the world where the Fathers sit.

68. Thou art the barhis of them that are our Fathers.

69. Loosen up the uppermost fetter from us, O Varuna, [loosen] down the lowest, off the midmost ; then may we in thy sphere, O Aditya, be guitless unto Aditi.

70. Release from us all fetters, O Varuna, with which one is bound crosswise, with which lengthwise ; so may we live hundreds of autumns, by thee, O king, guarded, defended.

71. To Agni, carrier of the Kavyds, [be] svadha [and] homage.

72. To Soma with the Fathers [be] svadha [and] homage.

73. To the Fathers with Soma, svadha [and] homage.

74. To Yama with the Fathers, Svadha [and] homage.

75. Here is Svadha for thee, O great-grandfather, and for them that are after (anu) thee.

76. Here is svadha for thee, O grandfather, and for them that are after thee.

77. Here is svadha for thee, O father.

78. Svadha to the Fathers that sit upon the earth.

79. Svadha to the Fathers that sit in the atmosphere.

80. Svadha to the Fathers that sit in the sky (div).

81. Homage, O Fathers, to your refreshment (urj) ; homage, O Fathers, to your sap.

82. Homage, O Fathers, to your terror * (bhama) ; homage, O Fathers, to your fury.

83. Homage, O Fathers, to that of yours which is terrible ; homage, O Fathers, to that of yours which is cruel.

84. Homage, O Fathers, to that of yours which is propitious ; homage, O Fathers, to that of yours which is pleasant.

85. Homage to you, O Fathers ; svadha to you, O Fathers.

86. They who are there, O Fathers — Fathers there are ye — [be] they after you ; may ye be the best of them.

87. They who are here, O Fathers — alive here are we — [be] they after us ; may we be the best of them.

88. Thee, O Agni, would we kindle, full of light (dyumani), O god, unwasting ; as that very wondrous fuel of thine shall shine in the sky (div), bring thou food for thy praisers.

89. The moon among the waters runs, and eagle in the sky (div) ; they find not your track, O golden-rimmed lighnings : know me as such, O firmaments (rodasi).

13
Conclusion

a. Religion-Dharma-Duty

With the realization of the fact that creation is an integral system, which is operating under a complex network of cyclic reactions, in which for every action there is a reaction in equal and opposite direction. Accordingly each and every component, has its own importance and duty in the system, the duties are under the universal laws. So to act in the society as per the mental development and quality of the work in the society is the Vedic-*Dharma*-duty. Which is having a motto of harmonious acts towards the nature and natural components. The same has been indicated in the Purusa sukta. Rg. 10.90, which became hereditary after the destruction of *the Vedic* civilization and the traditions, became the part of daily life.

Development of spiritualistic views of life and fear of God was not there during the Vedic period, after the *Brahaman Period*, which was flourished for about one thousand years, *after that Upanishad* period was there, which have established the philosophical view of life, accordingly six systems of philosophy *Shad-Darshan* came in to the light. With the entry of the foreign invaders, which were having an altogether different view about the Religion. They have interpreted the Religion in their own way.

The *Vedic* seers have laid down the foundation of customs and traditions, which were for the preservation of the knowledge but after the destruction of *the Vedic* culture, in the long due course of time the traditions became converted into the superstitions. The misinterpretations of the Vedic hymns have given it a different turn. In the same fashion after the foreign influence on India and the foreign rulers, who were believing in organized Religion, their concept of Religion was altogether different from the Indian concept of Religion, the Indian concept is related with the universal laws and to perform the duties according to the nature and quality of the work in the society is the Religion-Duty, hence there was no code or tradition for the change of Religion, but foreigners any how had compared it with their organized Religion, it was considered that the Indians have polytheistic approach towards the God, although to have a faith in God or not it is a personal thinking of a person concern in India. Foreigners have given it a name of *Hindu* Religion, which has divided the Indians in *the Hindu* and *Muslim*, although they belongs to the same country and having the same roots of origin being Indian. Here we should praise the intellectual supremacy and diplomatic policies of the Britishers that even after 57 years of the independence, we could not understand the British Policy and also could not find the solution for the unnatural Religious bifurcation, because India is unaware of its own culture, which is our weakness.

b. India and the Aryas

Another controversy, which involve the *Aryan* invasion in India can be solved through the Veda that the Vedic culture was a global culture after natural catastrophe and destruction, the Vedic culture restricted to India as the vast Geographical area has been described in the Veda, which is related with India, along with this there is no description of the Himalayan range of mountains.Because Himalayan range of the mountains came in to the existence after the Geological disturbances in post Vedic era.

The scientific facts revealed by the Vedic hymns about the knowledge of the Ozone layer, which protects the life on the earth. The presence of the magnetosphere around the earth and the magnetospheric processes, along with this the knowledge of the creatioin and its functions as an integral system. Through which the concept of *Vasudhaiv Kutumbakam*, the whole earth is one family came in to the existence, which includes every thing, which is present in the nature. These facts shows that the Vedic culture was a global culture, once in the history of the earth, without it such studies are not possible. It was only after natural catastrophe about 18000 years ago, with the ice age that the Vedic culture was restricted to the Indian subcontinent.

It is also a fact that in the long history of the earth once all the continents were united in one land mass known as *Pangea.* According to the *Wagner's theory of the continental drift,* due to the continental drift the land masses get separated from each other and the present continents came in to the existence.

It seems that after the natural catastrophe. Vedic culture was get restricted to the Indian sub continent, the natural situations forced them to live in the villages. Due to the natural Geological disturbances Himalayan range of mountains came in to the existence, where there was a *Tethy's* sea. In turn Vedic culture gets cutsoff from the rest of the world for a long time. On the journey for the new development as the barrier of Himalayan range of mountains was there on one side and on another side vast sea was there, accordingly world came to know about India after very long time that too through invaders and businessman only. One more thing that the different states of India are having different languages, customs and the traditions but the use of *Vedic mantras,* during ceremonies and rituals are the same, which is one of the important fact behind the preservation of *the Sanskrit* language and Vedic culture. On the contrary many languages like *Brahmi, Kharoshti, Pali, Prakrut* etc. have been vanished with time.

Jagatguru Adi Shankaracharya who has established the cultural integrity of India and has bind India in one cultural thread, it was also due to the *Sanskrit* and Vedic traditions, which are followed equally in all parts of India. Invaders cannot spread in each and every part, besides it is also a fact that in the Vedic culture there was no code for conversion of the people from other culture, the differences which were observed by the foreigners were due to the different branches of Veda. In the South India *Black Yajurveda* is common and in the north India *White Yajurveda* is common. Besides climate of the north India and south India are quite different, the north India is nearer to the hills and south India is nearer to the sea, accordingly due to the change in climate and temperature conditions a change in skin colour of the north Indians and south Indians is a natural phenomena. It is not a racial character as considered by the foreigners. One more thing is important that if *Aryans* came from out side of India than from where and why they came? There is no trace of it. Accordingly the theory of *Aryan* invasion and age of the Vedic culture should be analysed properly.

The Vedic traditional *Yajna*-sacrifice, may have some deep sense within it, because the whole creation is a *Srishti Yajna*, preparation of *Yajna vedi* signifies symbolically the stages through which the creation came in to existence. *Accordingly the chanting of **Mantra** and its sound with flames of fire from the Vedi must have some correlation, which should be analysed scientifically. As reported by the Scientists of Netherland that they have developed a technique to remove oil pollution through the use of sound waves. (New scientist vol.146)*

Purusa Sukta Rg. 10.90, is considered to be the latest among the hymns of *the Ṛgveda,* it seems that composition of the *Purusa Sukta* was there after having the full knowledge of the creation, which in a symbolic manner has established that human body is a microcosm inside a macrocosm, accordingly one can trace the truth through the self realization. It has given the way for the philosophy of *Upanishads,* after the destruction of the Vedic culture.The highest scientific truth regarding the creation and relevant development was not having correlation, the quest of the human mind to know about the mystery of the life on the earth was the quest of common people, accordingly the main trust area of the *Upanishads* is to establish the fact that the universal soul and the soul in the human body are one and the same.

c. Life and rebirth

The creation is working as an integral system, the system is self sufficient and self regulated.It is interesting to note that life on the earth is due to the ozone layer, which absorbs toxic ultraviolet rays in the upper atmosphere and acts as a shield for the living beings. The various forms of the living beings have been evolved from a single prokaryotic ancestor through evolution under space, time and environmental conditions.The biodiversity in the nature is due to the modification of the genetic sequence of the DNA. The life and death on the earth's surface is a natural phenomena under the process of evolution, Where human species is highly evolved showing evolution of the mental qualities with successive births, in this cycle the DNA carries the hereditary characters from one generation to another generation, which acts as a micro body of a person, which have the record of the deeds and the mentality in its language code. The thoughts and actions of a individual are in the form of a energy, as such the thoughts stored in a brain are beyond degradation, after the death of a individual they persist in the atmosphere. When the thought energy of a particular dead person finds its synonym language code on theDNA template of the embryo, accordingly the language get open. Which reflects the mentality of an individual with rebirth. When and where a individual mentality will take rebirth, it depends on the circumstances in which the person was living and his attitude towards the life, accordingly he has to bear the results of his past deeds with a new birth. A individual can proceed towards evolution through the contol on his mental emotions.

With such a scientific knowledge of the creation and nature the Vedas have been considered as *Apouresheya.*

14
Heritage-Asokan Emblem and the Wheel

Asokan emblem is the symbol of India's glorious past, which un fold the secret of the creation, which is not a myth or a product of intuition but a real experience of the Vedic culture, which was traced scientifically in a systematic manner under the space- time relationship as described in Vedic hymns. The same has been reflected in the Asokan emblem in an artistic way, which was found at Sarnath, where after enlightenment Lord Buddha delivered his first sermon. At the same place emperor Asoka placed this emblem along with the teachings of Buddha so as to commemorate his conversion in to Buddhism. From the same place it was taken as India's National emblem.

Irvin in his paper "*Origins of Forms and Structures*" has pointed out that Asokan emblem and pillars are the earliest stone monuments of India, they may be pre Asokan and some may be pre Mouryan. They are related with the cosmogonic myths related with the vedic versions. The testimony of the same can be traced in the *Puruṣa Sukta* Rg.10.90, where origin and the evolution of the creation has been traced from an fundamental energy, symbolically imaging it in the form of a *Purusa*, which explains the laws of Thermodynamics and cosmic principles, under which the creation is working as an integral system. The same has been projected in the Asokan emblem.

In the cosmogonic hymns of *the Rigveda* and *Atharvaveda*, the evolution of the creation has been traced from an fundamental energy with the name of *Visvakarma* Rg.10.81,

82. *Hiranyagarbha* Rg.10.121, *Prājapati* Rg.10.129 and *Puruṣa* in *Puruṣa Sukta* Rg.10.90. Which reveals the fact that the creation is a system, which came in to the existence from an fundamental energy through evolution with time, under which the nature exhibits its functions as a ecosystem, its components are synthesized under the temperature-pressure gradient (seasonal variations) and merged in the same with time through disintegration under natural cycles. Life is a integrated part of the nature, which exhibits its functions in a evolutionary manner, where the human beings are highly evolved showing evolution of the mental qualities under the cycle of rebirth and death (*Sankhya karika-Sankhya system of Philosophy*). The cyclic phenomena of the nature have been exhibited symbolically through *Chakra*-the wheel.

Sa Suryah paryuru varansyendro va vratyadrathyeva chakra. Rg.10-89-2

Surya is he; throughout the wide expenses shall *Indra* turn him, swift as car wheel, hither.

He drive the Sun and others like a wheel of the *Rath*-car. Which indicates about the working of the creation in a cyclic manner being driven by an fundamental energy.

Purusa Sukta

a. Modern Concept of Energy

All the Universe is energy, there is only energy, at some places energy get condensed in to the electrons, protons and neutrons, which bind together to produce atoms, and atoms in turn bound in to the molecules that produce substances, to whom we can touch, feel and call it as mass energy. In Einstein's equation $E=mc^2$ means energy and mass are interconvertible.

Our universe is a vast ocean of energy, where energy is working in a definite manner, which follows the laws of thermodynamics. Which state that energy is unborn and remains constant in all state, but energy can be converted from one form to another form with a successive loss of energy at every transfer. The energy can be defined as capacity to do work, in a object the energy at rest is known as potential energy. The energy at work is known as kinetic energy. Within the framework of these two energy, the all other fundamental forms of energy, such as the magnetic, electric, gravitational, heat and metabolic energy are working in the universe under the laws of thermodynamics. The laws of thermodynamics also state, when there is an increase it must be balanced by a decrease somewhere else. It means from energy point of view whole universe is a single unit we are only a small part of the same.

The same have been described in the Purusa sukta and has been depicted in the Asokan Emblem

b. Laws of Thermodynamics

Puruṣa Sukta deals with the laws of thermodynamics, where fundamental energy has been imagined in the form of a *Puruṣa* metaphorically, with having innumerable head, eyes and feet on every side, purvading the earth and the world he is enclosed in side a ten finger wide space, means as a universal entity the fundamental energy is present every where and as an individual entity he is enclosed in side a ten finger wide space, the region of the heart of man. Rg. 10.90.1.

Here it has been said that the *Puruṣa*-the fundamental energy is universally present.

This *Puruṣa* is all that yet hath been and that is to be;

The Lord of Immortality, which waxes greater still by food. Rg. 10.90.2.

Here it has been said that the fundamental energy is eternal, the lord of immortality means it can not be destroyed but with the transformation it increases, which is its food.

So mighty is his greatness; yea greater than this is *Puruṣa*. All creatures are one-fourth of him, three-fourths eternal life in heaven. Rg.10.90.3.

Here it has been said that the cosmos is like a vast ocean of the fundamental energy, the visible world is only one fourthpart of him and the rest three fourth part of it is in the heaven above the visible world.

With three fourths *Puruṣa* went up: one fourth of him again was here. Thence he strode out to every side over what eats not and what eats. Rg. 10.90.4.

Here it has been said that with its three fourth part invisible in the heaven, only its one fourth part is under going transformation again and again, which spread on every side as animate and inanimate creation.

Tracing the evolution from the fundamental energy symbolically in the form of a *Puruṣa*, with this it has been indicated that the human body is a microcosm in side a macrocosm.

c. Cosmic principles

In the last stanza cosmic principle of action and interaction has been given, under which creation is working as a system.

Gods sacrificing, sacrificed the victim: these were the earliest ordinances. The mighty ones attained height of heaven, there where the *Sadhyas*, Gods of old are dwelling. Rg. 10.90.16.

The *Yajna*-sacrifice means action and inter action, it has been said that from the action and interaction again action and interactions are get generated in which *Deva*-fundamental particles are the first according to the cosmic law. With their activity they reached to the height of the matter and *Deva*-fundamental particles. It means that initially the fundamental particles are the first in the series of reactions and the interactions, according to the cosmic principle through their activity they gets converted into the matter and reached to their original old state of *Deva*-fundamental particles, which indicates about the natural cycles through which the natural components are being synthesized and disintegrated in the reversible direction..

Seven fencing -sticks had he, thrice seven layers were prepared, When the Gods, offering sacrifice, bound, as their victim, *Puruṣa.* Rg. 10.90.15.

Here it has been said that the process of the creation has been started with the formation of *Deva*-the fundamental particles (electron, proton and neutron).

As the process of the creation has been started it was having seven sticks (seven planets), twenty one fuel were get prepared, these twenty one fuel are twelve months, six seasons and three weather through which the creation is working as an system having three centers-Sky, Atmosphere and the earth as indicated by the three layers.

d. Asokan Emblem

Asokan emblem has multidimensional characteristics. The pillar on which the emblem is placed along with the tapering lotus petals, it signifies that the pillar is the symbol of fundamental energy as a support to the creation as described in the *Skambha Sukta*, where the fundamental energy has been described as *Skambha*-the support. Ath. 10.7.35.

The radiating petals of lotus, signifies that the fundamental energy flows in to the existence like a lotus flower. Just like the branches of a tree round about the trunk. Ath. 10.7.38

The four lion back to back at the four cardinal points, they represents the fundamental energy in the vast oceon of the Cosmos.

The emblem having a circular shape, from the front only four legs and three faces of the lions are visible, the four legs indicates about the four parts of the fundamental energy out of which three fourth parts are above the visible cosmic world, the same has been indicated by the three faces of the lions.

Only one fourth part of the fundamental energy is undergoing transformation, which constitute the visible world, which is depicted at the base of the abacus represented by the four animals (Lion, Horse, Elephant and Bull) with the alternating wheel in between them.

To depict the four animals and the four wheels at the abacus, the each wheel has twenty four spokes. They symbolically represents various aspects of the creation.

Lion	The lion signifies the fundamental energy.
Horse	The horse signifies kinetic energy-energy of motion.
Elephant	The elephant signifies potential energy-energy at rest.
Bull	The bull signifies the capacity to do work.

The creation came in to the existence from an fundamental energy, through the actions and the interactions. The same has been indicated through the central axis, which represents the fundamental energy and the twentyfour spokes represents actions and interactions, the cyclic reactions have been indicated by the wheel. The four wheels alternating with the animals, each wheel is having a different significance for the creation system.

e. The wheel of Sun

The wheel represents the rotation of the sun at its axis, its one complete rotation is equivalent to a year of 360 days. The twentyfour spokes in the wheel represent twentyfour fort nights of fifteen days each, which is equal to 360 days. Rg. 1.164.48. It is the wheel of time-*Kala*, under which the creation came in to the existence.

f. The wheel of Nature

The nature is working as an system under twentyfour natural factors-forces as described in the Rg.10.65.1.

Agni, Indra, Varun, Mitra, Aryaman, Vayu, Pusha, Saraswati, 12 Aditya, Vishnu, Marut, Rudra and *Soma* are present in the nature along with the Lord of the creation. It is the wheel of nature.

g. The wheel of Seasons

The creation and nature are working as a system under seasonal variations as indicated in the Rg. 10.90.15. The twenty four spokes in the wheel represents twelve months, six seasons, three weather (winter-cold, summer-heat and Rain) and the three reaction centers the sky, atmosphere and earth. It is the wheel of the seasonal variations.

h. The wheel of Man

The twenty four spokes in the wheel signifies 24 elements of a man, five gross elements earth, sky, fire, water and air, five sense organs, five working organs of the body, five subjects of the sense organs, with this the mind, intellect, ego and nature develop gradually under the cycle of rebirth and death .(*Sankhya karika-Sankhya* system of Philosophy). The axis here represents the fundamental energy and the individual soul as the life principle, which indicates about the cycle of rebirth and death on the earth. It is the wheel of Man.

The central point in the wheel is its axis, which represent fundamental energy and as the spokes in the wheel have no importance without the axis in the same fashion the components of the nature and the creation have no importance without the fundamental energy. The same has been described as omnipotent, omnipresent and omniscient God in the various Religious scriptures, as such the National emblem is a symbol of National integrity and communal harmony with a pride and honor for the every Indian. It can form the bridge between the modern science and spiritualism, which is a quest of the modern human mind.

15
Astrology a Divine Science

Astrology is a branch of Astronomy through which human characteristics are determined on the basis of planetary positions in the horoscope. The zodiac chart is drawn for the moment of birth at a particular place, which shows the rising Ascendent at the time of birth and the degrees of the planets along with their cuspal position in different Sign-*Rashi*. The rising Ascendent in the horoscope represents the individual for whom the horoscope is being drawn.

Astrological principles are based on the planetary electromagnetic radiation influences, for which the birth chart provides the guidelines, the potency of influences depends on the degree of the planets and their Sign—*Rashi* in the cusp. (each cusp is divided in to degrees, minutes and seconds) In the solar system all heavenly bodies are moving rapidly around the sun, with rotation at their axis, accordingly the planetary positions and the potency of electromagnetic influence also get changed. Hence two individuals or 'time twins' can'nt have the same horoscope. The 'time twins' develop from the two different embryos or due to the cleavage of the embryo, which have different DNA, which decides the course of life through the hereditary characters and the code language of the DNA (De oxy Ribose Nucleic Acid), accordingly the genetic code language, which decides the future events of life will also get changed. Accordingly the living organisms and the climate get influenced by the planetary movements with their electromagnetic radiation potency, which differ according to the degrees of the planets and their sign-*Rashi* in the horoscope. 'Time twins' have difference due to the birth time, which may be from one minute and so on. The earth is moving around the sun at a speed of 29.79 km. or 18.51 miles per second with a time to reach sun light on the earth about 8.3 minutes and from moon about 1.3 seconds. Accordingly within a second the position of the birth place is also get changed, hence 'time twins' are having different planetary influences and time of events also get changed, which is responsible for the differences in the life of the 'time twins.'

In the horoscope, the position of the planets are given up to degrees, minutes and seconds, their daily motion around the sun and rotation at their axis can be determined through the sophisticated instruments, the same can be obtained from the Ephemeris but no instrument has been invented so far to asses the potency of the planetary electromagnetic radiation influences on the living beings. Zodiac chart drawn for the moment of birth is a miniature chart of the cosmos, it means a microcosm in side a macrocosm, which gives the guide lines to interpret the planetary influences on the person concern, through the planetary cuspal positions, which is not a machine its interpretations and the predictions are dependent on the capacity of the human mind, which require purity of mind and higher ethics in the life as the human mind is most sensitive, which can grasp the planetary electromagnetic radiation influences for the interpretation. Hence Astrology is being considered as a divine science, most of the predictions of the Astrologers are being failed because their mind are not so pure, due to the professional attitude in the life. In fact ethically Astrology must not be a professional tool, it is only useful and fruitful when utilized for the welfare of the human beings without any expectations. Such ethics in the modern life are not common, hence a pure divine science became the subject of professionals, who have devalued the Astrology, otherwise the Astrological principles are based on the Astronomy and electromagnetic radiation influences, which were laid down by the ancient *Vedic* scholars after having the full knowledge of the creation system. Under the cycle of the rebirth and death on the earth, where past deeds of an individual decides the fate in the present life, which can be judged from the 5th and 9th cusp-house of the horoscope.

Modern science is under the process of development, accordingly the new inventions are coming in the light but it will take time to have full knowledge of the creation system. Along with this without knowing the full principles and the ethics of Astrology to comment on it or to use it as a profession are responsible for the confusion among the intellectuals, due to which the common people are being misguided, otherwise Astrological principles can guide a person for better future within the limitations of his past deeds of his previous births, modern science is yet to touch the height of ancient scholars, from where the Astrological principles were laid down.

earth, where past deeds of an individual decides the fate in the present life, which can be judged from the 5th and 9th cusp-house of the horoscope.

Modern science is under the process of development, accordingly the new inventions are coming in the light but it will take time to have full knowledge of the creation system. Along with this without knowing the full principles and the ethics of Astrology to comment on it or to use it as a profession are responsible for the confusion among the intellectuals, due to which the common people are being misguided, otherwise Astrological principles can guide a person for better future within the limitations of his past deeds of his previous births, modern science is yet to touch the height of ancient scholars, from where the Astrological principles were laid down.

16

Origin of Life—Interdisciplinary Approach

a. Introduction

Life and death are two phenomena, which are going on alternately with time. Death is certain, because who so ever has taken birth, ultimately he will have to die and life is uncertain, which is temporary face during the evolutionary development of matter under space time and environmental conditions, it is like a ice berg in the sea water, having similar composition of H_2O but having different forms. It seems that life is a specific form of movement and energy, which emrge at a certain stage of evolutionary development of matter, which has acquired a specific form of energy transformation in a closed system.

Energy transformation, growth and reproduction are fundamental principles of life, which are common from unicellular to multicullular organisms. All forms of life are consists of cells and get originate from preexisting cells, they maintains their continuity through cell division, which shows continuity of life principle, which became complex with evolution. With the acceptance of the view that all life forms have been originated from preexisting cells only, it has given the importance to the quest as and when first life was originated on the earth.

b. Early History

Astronomical evidences indicates that earth came in to existinence probably 4.6 billions years ago, as a large cloud of extremely hot incandescent gas. Due to its extreme hot nature, it was belived that any trace of life could not be possible in these conditions. How ever with cooling of the earth's surface, after many thousands of years, life originated on the earth.

Geological findings shows that the rock of canadian precambrian rocks were having blue green algae, and bacteria, black charts of fig tree series in swaziland, Eastern transvaal shows the presence of filamentous srucutures re-asembling to debris. It has given the clue that the first life may have been originated about 2-3 billion years ago in the sea.

c. Chemical Clues to the Origin of Life

Modern researches have demonstrated the abiotic formation of organic subsatances in the early prebiological history of the earth. A.I. Oparin 1922, J.B.S. Haldane 1928 have suggested that the primitive atmosphere must have carbon dioxide, Ammonia, and Water vapour but no oxygens, Haldane claimed that such a Mixture, exposed to ultra violet rays would give rise to variety of organic compounds. Herold and Miller created a reducing atmosphere in a laboratory, they passed electric discharges throught the atmosphere and showed that methane, Ammonia and water can be converted in to Aminoacids.

Kensei, Kobayashi of Yokohama National University Japan had shown that high energy particles from space could have been convertd the gases of the earth's primitive atmosphere in to the molecules of amino acids.

According to Bungen Burg de Jong 1929, when two hydrophilic colloidal solutions carrying opposite charges are mixed, a viscous drops known as coaservates are often produced instead of continuous liquid phase. Oparin 1928 has suggested that these drops contain a number of particles of opposite charges held together by electrostatic attraction, there fore coaservates are regions of high concentrations of the two oppositely charged particles. A.I.Oparin 1968 obtained evidences that the Photosynthetic activity of porphyrin is get promoted when it is incorporated in coaservates.

Researches in the field of origin of life have demonstrated the prebiotic origin of ingradients of life, a gap which still exists between artificial models and initial living beings that how the life energy is get generated, which has provided the complexity to structural organisations and metabolism. Life is a temporary phase during the evolutionary development of matter, which is influenced by many factors, but life energy is unique. Once it has been generated it maintains its continuity throught replication.

d. The source of **Origin of Life.**

It seems that the life driving force and the seeds of origin of life were in the Primitive Solar nebula. It can be traced with the evolution of the universe and the planetary system.

The whole universe is filled with energy, there is only energy, in some places that energy condensed in to as electron, protons and neutrons, which bind together to produce atoms, and atoms in turn bound in to molecules that produce substances, to whom we can touch, feel and call it as mass energy. In Einstein's equation it is written as $E=mc^2$ means energy and mass are interconvertible.

Our universe is a vast ocean of energy, where energy under goes transfornmation, which follow the laws of thermodynamics. Which state that energy is unborn and eternal but energy can be converted from one form to another form with a successive loss of energy at every transfer. The energy can be defined as capacity to do work, the capacity with which it work is called potential energy. The energy at work is known as kinetic energy. Within the frame work of these two energy, all other fundamental forms of energy such as magnetic, electric, gravitational, heat and metabolic energy are working in the universe under the laws of thermodynamics, Behind the scene of universe there is fundamental energy. Laws of Thermodynamics also state that when there is an increase it must be balanced by a decrease somewhere else. It means from energy point of view whole universe is a single unit we are only a small part of the same.

In the beginning of the universe there is fundamental energy. That may be magnetic potential energy, which when came in to motion may have generated the electricity with dissipation of heat energy. Once the heat energy get in operation, it can produce charged particles, electron, proton and neutron. The nature of these particles is as such that particles with the same type of charge repel one another, and oppositely charged particles are strongly attracted. The movement of these particles may produce cloudy masses with a increase in their concentration and condensation, with this high temperature and pressure may have been generated which may be responsible for the formation of atoms and chain of nuclear reactions. In this way our primitive solar nebula may have been formed and the rotetary cloudy masses may have given the birth to our solar system. The cloudy masses with electron, proton, and neutrons, in the beginning these cloudy masses were extremely, incandescent gas.These incandescent gas clouds sattle in the universe according to the distance from solar nebula as per the decrease in temperatre. In accordance with the laws of motion and gravitation, they condensed to form planets. The heat generated by their contraction was sufficient to convert them in to moltan state, but not sufficient to initiate nuclear reaction in their centre.

As we know today that in our solar system, the planets are moving around the sun in an elliptical orbit. The planets are also rotating at their axis, due to their rotation they produce magnetic field and magnetosphere, which protects the planets from solar wind-the hot ionised plasma with magnetic field. The interplanetary space is field with plasma and having interplanetary magnetic field through which all the planets are interconnected.

e. Life on the Earth

To have a life on a planet, it seems that suitable temperature and availablity of water are most important. If a planet is nearer to sun water would evoporate and if it is farther away, water would freeze, in this respect the distance of the earth from the sun is important for the origin of life, which is neither very far from the sun, nor it is too close. Accordingly, under temperature pressure gradient and planetary movements earth and its atmospheric environmental conditions came in to existence, after a series of action and interactions, with time earth's incandesent cloudy gaseous mass cooled down in to liquid, with condensation of the same, a moltan mass was get formed, the moltan material then produced the rocky crust. The information which we are having today reveals the fact that below the rocky crust there is a semifluid magma-having two layers, which have formed the mantle. Below which a two layered core is pesent, the mantle is the seat of the earth quakes and volcanoes. Due to the wrinkling and shifting of underlying semi fluid magma the great crakes and mountains came in to existence. When earth cooled down sufficiently, with passage of time the oceans and lakes came in to existence. The rotation of the earth at its axis has developed an internal energy source, with this earth's magnetic field and magnetosphere came in to existence, which has provided a shield against solar wind. As we know that earth's atmosphere extend upto magnetopause, which acts as boundary between the earth and space. The magnetosphere is formed by the interactions of the solar wind particles-the electrons and protons, which constitute the hot ionised plasma, with sun's magnetic field. As a result of solar wind geomagnetic field interactions, mass momentum and energy are get transferred from solar wind to magnetosphere and complex pattern of several current systems have get generated in different parts of magnetosphere, which have provided electrical power for various magnetospheric processes, which under temperature pressure gradient influences the weather and climates on the earth. It means on the primitive earth suitable geological and atmospheric conditions for origin of life may have been generated due to the magnetospheric processes and chemical reactions under temperature pressure gradient and ultra violet rays.

The water molecules can brought hydrological cycle through evoporation and condensation. The water molecules in the presence of ultra violet rays can be dissociated into H^+ & OH^-. These OH^- ions with further dissociation can produce oxygen in turn it can combine with molecular oxygen to produce ozone molecules. In this way oxygen rich atmosphere with ozone layer may have came into existence. It seems that the universe under the influence of temperature pressure and cosmic rays is a big reaction centre in between sun and earth, the sun is the primary energy source for these atmospheric interactions. The earth has provided the cordial place for aggregatin of molecules and substances, where the gravitational force of the earth and its geomagnetism has played a significant role for evolutionary development of matter, which has provided the base for origin of life on the earth.

The evolution and development of matter, which leads to origin of life is mainly dependent on time factor, for which universal clock is set in the sun, which is related with the rotation of sun at its axis. When earth complets its one round around the sun, during that period sun rotates at its axis twelve times, these are its twelve faces which constitute twelve months, through which changes in temperature-pessure gradient and electron density is there in the universe, which causes the occurrence of seasons, which ultimately influence the development of matter and various chemical reactions on the earth. The planetary movement and rotation of sun and earth at their axis, with a fixed duration have given the concept of time as day-night, months, year and seasons, which is mainly responsible for changes in temperature- pressure and electron density in the atmosphere, which has triggered off number of chemical reactions in the region of ionosphere under the influence of cosmic rays, electric discharge and geomagnetic field of the earth. Consequently the different atmospheric layers came into existence, which has generated the cordial conditions for origin of life on the earth, the magnetosphere has provided the shield against high energetic solar wind, the ozone layer in the region of trophosphere has provided the shield against ultra violet rays. These are the preliminary conditions for origin of life, which may have been generated after millions of years, when earth came into existence and prior to the origin of life.

It seems that with the formation of solar system prior to the origin of life, Three energy centres have been developed, The sun, universe, and the earth. Nuclear reactions, conversion of hydrogen into helium and magnetic storms at sun's surface are the main energy source of the solar system. The interplanetary space of the universe is filled with hot ionised solar plasma, this interplanetary space is filled with interplanetary magnetic field and is the main centre for magnetospheric processes, which has generated the atmospheric gases, atoms and ions of molecules. The earth where aggregation of atoms, molecules and substances is there, under the gravitational and geomagnetic forces, it became the main centre for evolutionary development of matter, which has produced the basic ingradients for life. The first life has been originated in the deep sea with aggregation of molecules and formation of coaservative drops, consequently life may have been originated in two way manner with time.

On the one hand viruses may have been synthesized abiotically. As we know that viruses are tiny small obligate parasites, they are intermediate between the living and nonliving. They show properties of living beings only inside a living cell. It means they require fundamental life energy of which they are devoid off, which is present only in living cells. Normally the viruses are consist of nucleic acids surrounded by protein coat knows as capsid, which consist of capsomeres. But there are other types also, which are the membes of a group of myxovirus. They posses an outer membrane known as the envelope, which consist of lipid and protein and surrounds the capsid, Herpes also sometimes has an envelope. There is also a plant virus, potato tuber spindle virus, which consists of only RNA, without any protein coat and is transmissible and infectious.

The various forms of virus, shows evolutionary sequence in viruses. The viruses with only RNA may acts as base for genetic order during the evolution and origin of life, with the formation of coaservative drops. The coaservative drops contain viscous mass and charged particles showing movements in different directions. They are capable of absorbing substances and energy from the outside solution as open system do. The oppositely charged particles held together by electrostatic attraction in a closed system of coaservates, it may give it a rotatary movement, in turn it can exhibit the properties of living cell. As we know that streaming of protoplasm is an important factor, till the cell is showing streaming, it is considered as living and as soon as the streaming movements get arrest, the cell became dead. It means the streaming of viscous protoplasm inside the cell generates life energy. Once the coaserative drops have acquired the rotatary movements inside a closed system, in this condition virus like structure having only RNA (Ribose nucleic acid) (as potato tuber spindle virus), which may have been synthesised abiotically may infect or enclosed in such coaservates showing streaming, in this way first prokaryotic cell may have been originated on the primitive earth, which has maintained its continuity throught multiplication and complexity through mutation and evolution. It is also possible that the coaservates with energy transformation may get synthesise the genetic material at its own, through its various components.

The life energy is a electromagnetic energy, which has been generated due to the streaming movements of the viscous protoplsm in side a closed system. The life energy basically is the same, which was get generated initially in side the nabula, the same has shown its continuity in atoms, molecules, substances and in living beings through the formation of bond energy.

In the primitive conditions formation of nebula was there with interactions of energy and generation of charged particles, due to the movements of charged particles, magnetic energy gets generated. These charged particles with their opposite charges bind together to produce atoms, atoms consists of subatomic units-electron, proton and neutron. Electrons are extremely light having cloud like density of mass energy with a negative electric charge, protons are much larger in mass than electron and have a positive charge, neutrons have a mass energy equal to that of proton and are electrically neutral. Although other types of sub atomic particles have also been identified, but the properties of atoms and their ability to react chemically can be explained on the basis of these three elementary particles, which constitute the base of the whole nature.

In a atom positively charged protons and neutrons consitute the nucleus, around which vibrating clouds of negatively charged electrons move in elliptical orbits, due to the vibratory movements and spin of electrons, magnetic energy get generated. The magnetic energy with the electrostatic force of nucleus produces electromagnetic energy, which bind the atoms of similar nature. The atoms of diffrent elements can produce diatomic molecules, even polyatomic complex molecules and chains of thousand of atoms like RNA and DNA may get produced, which are the products of chemical interactions of the outermost electrons to yield chemical bond or a covalent bond, when two atoms share electrons or ionic bond, when electrons are transferred from one atom to another atom, it is the electromagnetic energy, which initiate the formation of bonds. Through these bonds the electromagnetic energy has maintained its continuity in atoms, molecules, substances and living beings. In the same manner it can be generated in closed systems of cellular organisms also through streaming of protoplasm, which has maintained its continuity through replication of cells, which gets complicated with the evolution of complex multicellular organisms. As can be seen in the human beings, which have three centre of electromagnetic energy. The individual cells have their own energy generating systems, which get connected together and constitute a electromagnetic circuit of the body. The heart which circulates the blood in the body is another centre for the generation of electromagnetic energy, which can be measured by electrocardiogram (ECG), the third centre is brain, its neuromotor apparatus through brain waves and neuromotive impulses generates electromagnetic energy in the body, which can be measured by electro encephalogram (EEG). Although these electromagnetic centres are different in their origin, but constitute a single unit and are coordinated by each other. Respiratory metabolism is its fuel and water is its base.

f. Conclusion

It is a fact that basic unit of life is cell. The life principle is hidden in streaming of protoplasm, which has acquired complexity and specification of cellular environmental conditions. At a first glance it looks that life on the earth is very complicated, because it get influenced by so many factors. But the whole universe is the manifastation of a single fundamental energy, which may be magnetic energy, with its various forms, it is working in the universe. Life on the earth is also its manifastation, where it has been enclosed in a closed system as life energy. Which initiate metabolic reactions along with electrostatic energy, which is commonly known as electromagnetic energy. In living beings untill it is bound and gets generated in a closed system, life is there, with ageing of the cells it gets disappear. Similarly the magnetic energy, which is being generated in the atmos, along with electrostatic energy of nucleus initiates the formation of molecules and substances. The complex subtances are produced under temperature-pressure gradient. Which have synthesised the prokaryotic cell in the beginning, which has maintained its continuity through multiplication. Once the genetic material has acquired the capacity to synthesise protein, the genetic code and mechanism of protein synthesis became complex and complex through mutation and evolution in different directions, consequently we have the biodiversity in the nature.

17
Vedanta Philosophy and Science

Nobody knows when life originated on the earth. It seems that several thousand years ago there was a culture as described in the vedas. It seems they had realized the existence of God and Soul and accordingly laid down the rules and regulations for the welfare of the society. Vedic culture was well versed in all the fields of knowledge as described in the vedas. With the natural course of time the vedic culture was get ruined and the vedic hymns were interpreted in a different ways. Accordingly our ancients described the etenal truth of the vedas known as vedant in the upnishads. The rules regulations and moral values described in the vedas and upnishads are according to the space, time and environmental conditions, as such they have little importance in the present environmental conditions. But the eternal truth, described in the vedas and upnishads is as true today as it was in past. Also the Vedic religion is the source of all religion. Eternal truth described in the upnishads is the eternal truth of all religion.

To teach the common people Vedic seers have correlated this eternal truth with the religion. Today in the religion there are so many frauds and falsehoods, due to this eternal truth also became under suspision. Accordingly scientists have established this fact that religion is based on faith and belief, it has no firm foundation. Modern science is based on the experiments observations and their results, as such scientists have no faith in God and religion. This has created a confusion regarding the axistence of God and soul. Faith and belief on God is a superstition. When people run towards materialism only they get frustration, for peace they run towards the spiritualism and they think that religion or spiritual guru will provide them the peace, but nobody has complete solution. Thus the common people are dwelling between religion and science, materialism and spiritualism.

Scientists are not prepared to believe that some thing is beyond science. They think that problems of the world can be solved through science. But without the help of spiritualism they can't solve the problems of the world. They can'nt create harmony between the human beings, on the contrary they have created jealousy, competition and frustration in daily life, humanity has no role in the life.

Modern scientists believe only in the physical senses, which provide us a sense for looking at the universe, but no one knows how much of the real universe is lying beyond our physical senses. On the contrary vedas and upnishads say that when a person closes doors of his physical senses, he would be able to see beyond. The Vedic seers and saints have attained this stage and have established this fact that God is present everywhere in the universe in the plants, animals and the human beings be harmonized with them. Every thing present on the earth is for wise utillization. We have forgotten this fact and consequently we are facing environmental crisis and frustration in daily life.

To have a faith in God is superstition God is invisible, Vedic seers have described God as supernatural power, which has no shape and looking everywhere in the universe.The Soul and God are similar, which are invisible minutest having no smell, nor it can be divided further till the soul is there life is there, when soul moves out of the body death is there, and soul can take rebirth.

In the present circumstances all these sayings are meaninglerss, because we believe only on those things, which can be realized by our physical senses. If we concentrate on above sayings in the lights of this that our culture was great culture and our ancients were not fools. If they have laid down certain facts in the books, it must have certain meaning and due to the natural course of time facts are hidden and covered by certain false beliefs.

If God or soul has any existence, it must have certain form. If we consider the above sayings in the light of modern science then we may reach nearer to the truth.

Modern physics has very high place among all the sciences because in physics one can conduct very minute experiments. Certain elementary particlas have been discovered during last 80 years among them are electron, proton, neutron, positron, muons and neutrino etc.

Among these elementary particles neutrino is very unique, Pauli 1931 has suggested the existence of neutrino and farmi given a detailed theory. Its existence was accepted merely to save law. Physicist considered it only the ghost of a particle. Only in 1953 Clyde L Cowan and frederick Reines discovered it indirectly. This particle neutrino is massless, uncharged and travel constantly at the velocity of light and can penetrate endless thickness of dense matter. It interacts very weakly with other particles and hence very difficult to catch it. When it interact with any particle its existence came to an end and it produces another particle, this new particle produces characteristic tracks and lines on photographic plates. Only from these indirect inferences one can say that neutrino has been found. Interaction of neutrino with other particles is very rare only one out of million photographic plates may show up its existence. But today if one wants to prove the existence of neutrino, he will require many years along with deep study of physics and related subjects for understanding the meaning of lines. Even though he may not be able to confirm the existence of neutrino but he can'nt deny the theories.

Similarly electron theory proposed by Niel's Bohr 1913. Electrons are considered to be the minutest and can't be divided further, its presence can be detected by the charactenstic tracks and impressions on the photographic plates. Many theories in physics, Chemistry, and Biology are based on this electron theory.

As in Physics, Chemistry and Biology various theories have been based on the existence of neutrino and electron, similarly the moral rules described in the vedas and Upnishads were based on the existence of God and soul. The eternal truth described in vedas and Upnishads can't be denied as it was being observed by our ancients and they have sacrifice their lives after it.

If we consider God and soul on above line then neutrino, which interact very rarely is God and its impression on photographic plates is the soul which is universally present in the universe.

Soul as described by our ancient saints is minutest it can'nt be divided further, its presence can be realized during meditation in the form of flame and light. For meditation they have prescribed Ashtang yoga the eight disciplines. Now the question arises that if the soul is minutest why flame and light is visible?

We can compare soul with electron. Niel's Bohr who has given the theory of electron says that these electrons are invisible and in normal condition they are in bond state. When energy get induced they jump from the one orbit to another orbit, during the transition of electrons from higher to lower energy levels, they may release energy as visible light or other wavelengths of radiation.

During the meditation followed by eight disciplines, when one closes doors of his physical senses, mind will be empty of thoughts, waves of mind will be still in that state, he can realize the light of soul. For attaining this state, one will require a long period of meditation depending on the nature of the person concern.

During meditation when one concentrates continuously on one object sufficient amount of energy is induced in the brain. Due to this electrons present there in transists from one orbit to another orbit and consequently different wave lengths of radiation are emitted, when all the wavelengths are emitted white light is there. Simultaneously due to continuous concentration there are certain chemical changes in the brain, due to which universal sky of infinite mind appears and light is visible. The electrons reveals the different pictures, depending on the depth of conciousness. As these electrons are associated with brain and present there till the body is alive, its confirmation is quite difficult but modern physicist may prove it in future.

When one who will realize the presence of these electrons will see God everywhere, it means that he will feel that invisible factor which is present in his body is present everywhere in the universe as well as in the plants, animals and other humanbeings.

Our ancients have realized this fact accordingly they have described eternal truth and cited that plants, animals and human beings are your fellow beings be harmonized with them. This eternal truth is for the welfare of all living beings. When people will realize this fact that all human beings are the sailors of the same boat, they will feel harmony and sympathy for each other, humanity and peace will be everywhere on the earth. Without the humanity modern scientific development is useless.

18
Divine Light and Soul

It is common concept among the people that religions are antagonistic, due to this communal riots are there. But it is not so all religions are basically humanistic, to spread the seeds of humanity, the religious scriptures have given moral codes. These moral codes are according to the space, time and environmental conditions some of the moral codes which where applicable at the time of origin of religion, due to the environmental conditions of that time. These are still persisting even though the environmental condition have changed a lot, people are follwing these things treditionally. These traditions sometimes create disharmony between the people of different religions and faiths, consequently communal riots are there. Sometimes due to the superstitions and orthodox nature of some people riots are there among the people of same religion and community also.

Religions have originated long back in different environmental and Geographical conditions, when land and people were separated from each other Geographically and socially, as the adequate facilities for the transport and communication were not available. The fundamental concepts and nature of God and soul in all religions is the same. It means that all the prophets and the saints have realized the same thing; and the difference in the moral codes is only due to the environmental conditions of that time. The followers of each religion should think deeply that due to the modern scientific development rapid communication and transport facilities are there, now the world is one and we have to leave together, otherwise whatever we have earned to day will be destroyed.

Our saints and prophets were great philosopher and thinker we have regarded them God. Beacause they have given us a way of living life through humanity, although they were people like us.

Concept of humanity in the religions is due to the existence of God and soul, which is same in all the religions. It means our ancient prophets and saints were of the same category and thinking. Due to our low nature and thinking, we are not understanding them.

If we at all consider the existence of God, than there can'nt be two God. If he has blessed us with extraordinary things then he has also blessed others with the same, defect is there in our thinking.

In all religions existence of the soul in the body has been accepted, simultaneously they say that soul is representative of God. It means every human being is God and if we give trouble to any human being by our doings then we are giving trouble to God. In our day to day life we are not following this. We are following only the traditions in which our interests are safe; in this way we are exploiting the religion as well as ourselves because the soul which is present in ourselves by our wrong doing get spoiled, it means vibrations of our wrong thinking covered the soul, soul in it self is pure, after death either it will go to hell or it will take re-birth in to a low class family or in a animal world. The present era is era of science. Modern scientific development has established this fact that science is supreme, as secientists were unable to prove the existence of soul. We have accepted that no hell, no heaven and no rebirth, but whenever our interests are affected we use the name of God and soul for our selfishness. If we at all have a faith in religoin then we must have a faith in God and soul, which have a scientific background, that too realized by our ancient saints and prophets in a similar manner through meditation.

In all religions, it is accepted that soul is life energy, which is invisivble, eternal but present in the body as representative of God, it is in the form of light as shining flame. Those who are dutiful, truthful and not involved fully in materialistic life they can realize this light.

In Upanishads soul has been regarded as the minutest indivisible, invisible by naked eyes but its presence can be realized through meditation in the form of flame and light.

In Quran prophet *Mohammad* says that soul is present in the body. In *sura Kaf* he says that everyperson came with a driver and a witness and when he says that God (*Allah*) is very close to you even closer then the vein of your neck, it means that soul is within you. Further he says that those perosns who are dutiful, who are on right path they can realize the light of God (*Allah*). Description of this type of light is there in *Sura-Us-Shums* (Sun) prophet Mohammad has given the example of this light how it shines in dutiful and truthful persons. In *Sura-Un-noor* where he says that "it is like that, that in side a glass chamber there is a shining star, though no fire or light touch it but it kindled from a blessed tree". This light does not require any external source. God (Allah) guided those who follow right path in this manner.

In Bible saint Jesus Christ says that soul is present in the body, soul is flame of God.

In new testament (6-22) saint Mathew says that light of the body is eye, if thine eye be single your body will be full of light. But if thine eye be evil, thy whole body will be full of darkness. (New testament 6-22).

Saint paul says that your body is temple of God. God is inside you.

Iniades desceibe that aim of soul is to touch the soul not by any onter light but by its own light.

J Boehme and willium law have realized the soul in the form of divine light.

Prophet Zarthustr in Zend-Avesta has also recognised the soul in the body. He has realized the divine fire in the body means light.

It means all the prophets and saints have recognised the existence of soul and its presence can be realized in the form of light. Consequently all religion says that God is light.

If all religions say same thing than it must have firm background although modern scientists say that soul is matter of faith and belief, we may consider that traditions and customs are the matter of faith and belief as they are different in different religions, but nature of soul its method of realization through meditation and truthfulness is same in all the religions, it is the matter of concentration whether it is scientific or not.

Ancient saints in the upanishad have written that soul is minutest, indivisible, and eternal it means, if it is present it is a form of energy, which is different from the other forms known to us. In all religions it has been accepted that the presence of soul can be realized in the form of light and flame. Now the question arises how the flame and light is visible.

If we corelate the above things with the theory of atomic structure we may get a suitable answer. Atom as postulated by John Dalton is minutest indivisible solid sphere. Niels Bohr 1913 has proposed the atomic structure according to him in a atom there is a nucleus in the centre and electrons move around the nucleus. These electrons are negatively charged particles and responsible for the conduction of electric current.

According to the theroy of atomic structure. electrons are invisible in normal conditions as they are in bond state, when energy is induced they jump from the higher to lower energy levels, during transition of electrons from one orbit to another orbit, they may release energy as visible light or other wavelengths of light.

Ancient saints and prophets may have realized the light in above manner, when one concentrates continuously on one abject sufficient amount of energy is induced in the brain due to this energy, the electrons present there in transists from one orbit to another orbit and consequently different waevelengths of radiations are emitted and when all the waveleneths are emitted white light is visible. Simuitaneously due to the continous concentration, there are certain chemical changes in the brain, due to which universal sky of infinite mind appears and light is visible.

Explanation for the Divine Light

Upanishads have regarded that in the brain there is a cavity which is the seat of the soul and the presence of soul can be realised through meditation in the form of light and flame. Normally, when eyes are open we see things, light and light patterns because light falling on the retina of the eyes, stimulates the eye cells there in to produce electrical signals, through optic nerves these signals reaches in the vision centre of the brain cortex, it excites the cells there in and we perceive light, in the body the eyes are working like a camera and produces images in the vision centre, simultaneously there are certain chemical changes in the brain and the image is realised. It is not always necessary for light to fall on retina to stimulate brain cortex. A small amount of residual electrical activity occurs in the cortex also whether the stimulation of retina is there or not. Due to this when we hit eyes or head with hammer or by any object, the residual electrical activity leaks in to the vision centre of the cortex and stimulate the cells, thus we perceive briefly, some flashes of light and stars. The vision is anamolous, it is evident from the fact that it is not the same in case of repeated hitting of the head or eyes.

It seems that during meditation and concentration followed by *Ashtang yoga* (the eight disciplines), a gradual stimulation of nerves of nervous system from *Muladhar Chakra* (the base of spinal cord) up to the *Sahasrar Chakra* (mid brain) is there. Due to the stimulation of the nervous system electrical activity is initiated in the brain, which when leaks in to the vision centre of the brain, it brought chemical changes, accordingly the light of different wavelengths are visible, although the eyelids are closed. Stimulation of the nerve cells of the nervous system also influences the electro magnetic currents in the brain, due to which excited charged elementary paricles are also produced, these charged elementary particles emitts different wavelengths of light in the vision centre of the brain in the same fashion as atmospheric auroral displays are there during night. Which appears during the disturbed magnetic field conditions in the atmosphere.

Similarly with continuous meditation and concentration practises, a change in the human body's magnetic field is also there, which may be the cause of divine light.

It may be possible that in above manner the ancient saints and prophets may have realized the soul. Accordingly they have given the concept of divine light, all the saints and prophets can't be wrong.

With the realization of soul they might have realized that on the earth every thing is working in a definite manner on which man has no control, the force, which is invisible and unexplainable, which is beyond the imagination of common people, so they have corelated it with God.

God as explained by ancient saints in Upanishads and by the prophets is very much similar.

Commonly they have described that God is eternal, invisible, present every-where, he is greater than greatest, due to his will Sun, moon and stars are shining. He is the king of universe. He is shapeless. He is the creater, he is the destroyer, every thing is under his control. It means that at distant places the saints and prophets have realized the same thing.

If we are quarraling for our false beliefs and customs unknowingly we are giving pain to our God, if we at all believe in God? God can'nt be different for different people, only names are different due to different languages.

If we want to leave on earth, we must visualize that what is wrong and what is right, which is applicalbe to all, we cannot force others to accept our views. Whatever we think is always not correct. It seems that the nature of the God, which has been described by the religious scriptures is similar as omnipotent, omnipresent and omniscient, which indicates that they are drawing attention towards the fundamental energy, from where the creation came in to existence through energy transformation. It is also a fact that energy and mass are inter convertible as suggested by the great scientist Albert Einstein in his equation $E=mc^2$ means the energy and mass can be converted in to each other.

19
References

Agrawal V.S. Sparks from the Vedic fire, School of Vedic Studies, B.H.U. Varanasi.

Albanese Ancient India: From the origins to the XIII Century A.D. By Marilia Albanese, Om Book Service, Delhi

Bernal, J.D The Origin of Life, Weidenfield and Nicholson, London, 1967.

Bhatnagar, M.S. The Concept of Matter and its status in IndianLiterature, IJHS, 191 V 125-42-1984.

Bloomfield Religion of the Veda.

Bloomfield Athrvaveda and Gopath Brahamin, Chaukhamba Vidhya Bhawan, Kashi.

Chawla The Rigvedic Deities and their Iconic Forms, Jyotsna Chawla, MRML

Devitt, W Biology of the cells, An Evolutionary Approach, W. B. Saunders, company, London.

Fox, S. W.(ed). The Origin of Life prebiological System and of their Molecular structure, Academic press, New York, 1965

Gaud, P.N. The exact Sciences in Veda, IQJM 91 V 237-51-1919.

Griffith Hymns of Rigveda, Motilal Banarsidas, New Delhi.

Gupta, M. L.	Truth about the Solar system as revealed in Rigveda. BSSS 42 IV 1974-75.
Haldane J.B.S.	The Origin of Life, The Rationalist Annual, 1929.
Irvin	Origins of Form and Structures
Jha V.N.	Metaphors in Vedic Literature, Editor V.N. Jha, CAS in Sanskrit, University of Pune, Pune.
Keith	The Development and History of Sanskrit Literature, Sanjaya Prakashan, Delhi.
Lokesh Chandra	Dictionary of Buddhist Iconography in 2 Vols. International Academy of Indian Culture and Aditya Prakashan, Delhi.
Maxmuller	History of Ancien Sanskrit Literature, Panini Office, Allahabad.
Maxmuller and Kieth	Vedic Index.
Macdonell and Keith	Vedic Index on Names and Subjects, ChaukhambaVidhya Bhawan, Kashi.
Mcdonell, A.A.	Vedic Reader for students, Oxford University press, London.
Mcdonell, A. A.	History of Sanskrit Literature, Munshi Ram Manohar Lal, Nai Sarak, Delhi.
Mcdonell, A.A.	Vedic Mythology.
Nason, A.	The biological world, John Wiley & sons Inc. NewYork.
Oparin, A.I.	Modern Concepts of the Origin of Life on the earth, Recent Development in plant Science, Today and Tomorrow Printers and Publishers, New Delhi.
Parker, E.N.	Cosmical magnetic fields, their Origin and activity, Clarendon Press, Oxford. 1979.
Parkinson, W.D.	Introduction to Geomagnetism, Scottish Academic press, Edinbrgh.

Rao, M.S.N.	New Interpretation of Indian Art and Culture, Editor, Kusumanjali.
Robertis E.D.P.	Essentials of cell and Molecular Biology, Halt Saunders, Japan.
Tewari S.P	Hindu Iconography, Agam Kala Prakashan, Delhi.
Thatte, A.P.	The mighty little atoms, Basic Sciences, IBH Publishing company.
Upadhya, B.	Vedic Sahitya and sanskrati, Sharda Mandir, Varanasi.
Volland, H.	Atmospheric Electrodynamics, Springer, New York, 1984.
Weber, Albrecht	The History of Indian Literature, Chaukhamba Sanskrit Series Office, Varanasi.
Whitney. W.D.	Atharvaveda Samhita, Translation in 2 Vols., Motilal Banarsidas, Delhi.
Wilson	Rigveda Samhita, English Translation, Munshi Ram Manohar lal, Nai Sarak, Delhi.